CALIFORNIA'S
CHANGING ENVIRONMENT

CALIFORNIA'S CHANGING ENVIRONMENT

Raymond F. Dasmann

series editors:
Norris Hundley, jr.
John A. Schutz

Boyd & Fraser Publishing Company
San Francisco

CALIFORNIA'S CHANGING ENVIRONMENT

Raymond F. Dasmann

Manufactured in the United States of America.

Library of Congress catalog card number: 81-66064

ISBN 0-87835-116-7

2 3 4 5 · 5 4 3 2

EDITORS' INTRODUCTION

MENTION THE NAME CALIFORNIA and the popular mind conjures up images of romance and adventure of the sort that prompted the Spaniards in the 1540s to name the locale after a legendary Amazon queen. State of mind no less than geographic entity, California has become a popular image of a wonderful land of easy wealth, better health, pleasant living, and unlimited opportunities. While this has been true for some, for others it has been a land of disillusionment, and for too many it has become a place of crowded cities, congested roadways, smog, noise, racial unrest, and other problems. Still, the romantic image has persisted to make California the most populated state in the Union and the home of more newcomers each year than came during the first three hundred years following discovery by Europeans.

For most of its history California has been shrouded in mystery, better known for its terrain than for its settlers—first the Indians who arrived at least 11,000 years ago and then the Spaniards who followed in 1769. Spaniards, Mexicans, and blacks added only slightly to the non-Indian population until the American conquest of 1846 ushered in an era of unparalleled growth. With the discovery of gold, the building of the transcontinental railroad, and the development of crops and cities, people in massive numbers from all parts of the world began to inhabit the region. Thus California became a land of newcomers where a rich mixture of cultures pervades.

Fact and fiction are intertwined so well into the state's traditions and folklore that they are sometimes difficult to separate. But close scrutiny reveals that the people of California have made many solid contributions in land and water use, conservation of resources, politics, education, transportation, labor organization, literature, architectural styles, and learning to live with people of different cultural and ethnic heritages. These contributions, as well as those instances when Californians performed less admirably, are woven into the design of the Golden

State Series. The volumes in the Series are meant to be suggestive rather than exhaustive, interpretive rather than definitive. They invite the general public, the student, the scholar, and the teacher to read them not only for digested materials from a wide range of recent scholarship, but also for some new insights and ways of perceiving old problems. The Series, we trust, will be only the beginning of each reader's inquiry into the past of a state rich in historical excitement and significant in its impact on the nation.

Norris Hundley, jr.
John A. Schutz

CONTENTS

CHAPTER ONE

The Way Things Were

NOT LONG AGO the earth seemed a more stable place than it is today. It was possible to write about California with assurance from geologists that this piece of the planet had been sitting right where it is since the continents first took shape. True, it had its ups and downs—sometimes flooded by the Pacific Ocean, sometimes high and dry with taller mountains and deeper canyons than we live with at this time. At least it was here, somewhere between 32 degrees and 42 degrees latitude north of the equator, and mostly between 115 and 124 degrees of longitude west of Greenwich. But we no longer have that assurance since geologists began speculating that Alfred Wegener and his theory of continental drift might not be insane after all. Now we no longer know for sure where California was at any point in geologic time, and furthermore we think a fair-sized piece of California is not strictly speaking part of North America at all.

Our land, back in the days of giant amphibians and forests that were to become coal, nestled with other continents near the South Pole. By the time the dinosaurs were wandering about, the continents were on the move, each riding on its lithospheric plate, a solid rock base which could slide over the more molten layers of magma below. The American plate coming from the east encountered the Pacific plate, on which the ocean rides, in the area we now call California. The meeting place, marked by

the San Andreas fault, is the main source of California's earthquakes because the American plate tries to move westward
while the Pacific plate slides in a more northerly direction.
Something gives, and the state shakes a little, or a lot, each time
it does. Those of us who live to the west of the fault will be
moved northward and may have to say goodbye to America
whether we would like to or not. But that event will occur millions of years into the future, and we are here concerned with
more immediate time.

California is an unstable land of volcanoes and earthquakes,
of shifting coastlines and mountains that have come and gone.
Long before people became an environmental force of any consequence, there were days when the air was dreadfully polluted
from volcanic fumes and when fish died in waters poisoned by
toxic wastes brought to the surface by natural forces. But these
occurred in infrequent times of disaster, memories of which
were passed down in the legends of the first Californians.

During most of the years when people were in this land, California was a place unusually favorable to the support of a great
diversity of plant and animal life. This variety in combination
with the prevailing mild climate made it a favorable place for
people. It was a place where more people could live better while
doing less of what we usually call work than in most other parts
of the United States. It still is.

We may never know when the first human beings appeared in
California. There are no legends of their coming. The original
people of California believe that they sprang from the earth
right here and that they have always inhabited these western
lands since the world was created. Certainly the duration of
human occupancy has been pushed back far enough that the
theory of the movement of American Indians from Asia to
North America during the last glacial age, 15,000 plus or minus
years ago, is at least open to question. Some people undoubtedly came from Asia across the Bering land bridge at that time,
but they may have arrived in a continent settled long before.
Radiocarbon dates which suggest human occupancy of Santa
Rosa Island more than 29,000 years ago no longer seem unreal-
istic.[1] If people were on Santa Rosa then, how did they get
there, from where and when? Were they part of another Asiatic
migration? We have no final answer.

It is useful to reconstruct the human story of the California islands since these were not only areas with a long record of human population, they were also densely populated, by comparison with most other regions of the state, before Europeans arrived. They are today recovering from severe environmental degradation resulting from activities carried on by European colonists. If we accept the presence of early Californians on the Channel Islands 30,000 years ago, we must also acknowledge that their environment was greatly different. The northern Channel Islands, from Anacapa to San Miguel, were joined in some way. Their climate was wet and cool. Redwood, douglas fir, tan-oak and madrone forests were present, similar to those of the Santa Cruz Mountains today—200 miles farther north. Large cypress trees, at least two feet in diameter, were to be found on the islands. A dwarf mammoth was present (*Parelephas exilis*) and was hunted and butchered by the people. Perhaps their main foods came from the sea where a variety of sea mammals and birds were abundant, along with large numbers of abalone—a highly preferred shellfish in more recent Indian diets. We know little about the effects of these people on their environment. They may have exterminated the mammoth—the last remains are dated from 11,800 years ago. In any event, the mammoth is unlikely to have survived the drying of the climate and the shrinking of the land area of the islands as sea levels rose at the end of the ice age.

About 7,500 years ago a recognizable culture could be identified from its artifacts. These people, the Dune Dwellers, lived in villages by the shore. A dry climate may have restricted the productivity of upland vegetation and forced great reliance on sea food, particularly red abalone. Perhaps 5000 years ago a different cultural sequence appeared. Sea levels became somewhat higher than today. Certainly the oceans grew warmer, since the black abalone replaced the red. The climate became cooler and moister, so that forests spread. People moved into the uplands where acorns, seeds, and tubers were their principal foods. These people of the Highlander culture kept to their ways until the return of another dry period, starting perhaps 3000 years ago. During that time, the latest, or Canalino culture took shape, oriented toward the sea, leaving great shell mounds of black abalone and sea mussels, capturing sea turtles, and leaving baskets of sea grass. This final cultural phase was one of great seafaring ability—with canoes built from planks of Torrey pine, Monterey pine, or Bishop pine.

Relating these cultural phases to the ethnic groups to be found in California at the time of European settlement has not been done satisfactorily. Coastal southern California may have been first settled by Hokan-speaking peoples, the Chumash, who occupied the islands and are clearly the people of the Canalino culture. Sometime around 500 B.C. Uto-Aztekan-speaking peoples from the Great Basin reached the coast and settled the area from Los Angeles to northern San Diego County, establishing a wedge between the Chumash and their Hokan-speaking counterparts, the Diegueño of the San Diego area. These Uto-Aztekans, referred to as the Gabrielinos (after Mission San Gabriel), also occupied Catalina and San Clemente islands. However, far out on San Nicolas Island, the Nicoleños may have spoken a language which could not be understood by their island neighbors.

What do we know of these peoples and their environmental relationships? Their word for god was Chinigchinich, and they used the dangerous hallucinogen *Datura* in their religious ceremonies. They had a reverence for the spirits of animals—Coyote, the sacred trickster god; ravens, the messengers of the gods; dolphins, who patrolled the boundaries of the world and kept it safe for men. That they used fire and used it to a purpose—keeping the oak groves (their acorn orchards) open and more accessible; helping with their hunting—we know. They hunted the abundant sea otter and made cloaks from its skins, but left it as abundant as before. Despite their seafaring ability they did not travel far. Like most California Indians they tended to remain at home, and this sedentary way of life accounts in part for the remarkable diversity of people in California at the time of European settlement.

There were six major language groups of California Indians, divided into more than 50 little nations and 250 or more tribelets usually speaking different dialects. There were more than 300,000 people in the state; a denser population than in any area of comparable size in the United States. Yet these people lived "off the land"—hunting, gathering, and fishing. Except for the desert groups along the Colorado River, they had no agriculture, and none had domestic herd animals. They lived well because the land was rich, its plant foods abundant, and its native animal life prolific. The first of the Californians may be represented by the Yukian peoples after whom Ukiah is named. They lived in Napa, Lake, and southern Mendocino counties. Their language was unique, and they were of a different physical appearance from their neighbors. Also long present in the state were the Hokan-speaking people who extended from the Shastan group in the north to the Yumans in the south. The distribution of the Hokans is disrupted by what may have been a group of later arrivals, the Penutian-speaking peoples who occupied the San Francisco Bay and Monterey area, the Central Valley and the northern Sierra. Perhaps still later the Algonkian and Athabascan peoples came into the state and occupied the north coast—people with affinities in the Pacific Northwest. At some point, the Uto-Aztekan group moved into the Great Basin side of the state and spread across the Mojave Desert to the southern California coast.

The lands that the Indians occupied differed from the lands of California today. One major difference is in the distribution of water. From the Feather River in the north to Bakersfield in the south the Central Valley of California was a valley of marshes. Tules, cattails, and other water plants occupied a large area, as much as 50 miles across, along the banks of the Sacramento and the San Joaquin rivers. During winter and spring floods large areas of the Central Valley were covered with water. Tulare Lake in the south was nearly four times the area of Lake Tahoe although shallow, and south of it Buena Vista and Kern lakes were sometimes joined in a lake perhaps as large as Mono Lake—which was itself overflowing with water. There was no Salton Sea, only an alkali flat, the Salton Sink, occasionally holding water after desert rains. San Francisco Bay was larger and surrounded by extensive salt marshes—mostly long since filled in.[2]

The vegetation was different. The California annual grasslands, which contribute the golden look in summer to this "green and golden" state, were not there. Grasslands there were, but of a different nature—tall, perennial bunch grass prairies, thick and spongy underfoot. Forests were both more extensive and more open, without the dense tangles of brushy undergrowth. Riparian woodlands of hardwood, deciduous trees occupied large tracts of ground along the Sacramento–San Joaquin system and its tributaries, above and surrounding the marshes. Open oak savannas were more widespread, chaparral much less so than today. People were to be encountered here and there, never in large numbers, but their influence was not to be ignored.

The role played by the California Indians in the extermination of the Pleistocene fauna may long be debated.[3] With the possible exception of isolated and already declining species, such as the dwarf mammoth, there is no strong evidence that early California people contributed to the extermination of any animal. However, invading species invariably have more serious disruptive effects upon an established biota than they will have after a period of establishment. The first Polynesians to invade New Zealand exterminated the giant flightless birds, the moas, which had lived there previously. Later the Maori culture lived in balance with the other animal and plant species of those islands. Similarly, the first Californian hunting people, arriving in areas where animals had no knowledge of—or defenses against—humans, may have had a much more serious effect upon populations of ground sloths, cave bears, saber-toothed cats, mammoths, and mastodons than could be believed from consideration of the near-symbiotic human-animal relationship that later developed.

At the time of European settlement the wild animal life of California was at a level of diversity and abundance almost unbelievable today. Not only were species which have since become extinct still abundant—the California grizzly, for example—but most species had a much more extensive range than they have today. Furthermore, the behavior of animals was different. They lacked the fear of man that was to be essential for their survival after the Europeans.[3] Those that were most fearless were to die.

Perhaps the greatest effect that the early California people had upon their environment was through the use of fire. From all evidence, fire was as much a factor in the California scene as was the Mediterranean-type, summer-dry climate that favored its spread. The Indians burned to aid in hunting, and to encourage those plants they used for food, medicine, and other purposes. One might say that they tended the vegetation in the lands that they occupied over thousands of years to create a favorable home environment—to keep the forests more open, to encourage the increase of deer, and to favor the production of acorns. To some degree the pre-European California landscape was created by the interaction of humankind and the natural world—or at least that was true in the areas that were settled. The territory of the tribelet was definitely tended—but beyond that was the wild land. There were places where no human had been. Despite all the changes, there may still be such places.

There are six major biotic provinces in California, areas which are sufficiently distinct in fauna, flora, and vegetation to be recognizably different from each other—the Oregonian, of tall redwood and douglas-fir forests, extends from the Pacific Northwest to San Francisco Bay on the seaward side of the high coastal ranges; the Sierran-Cascade, in the high north coastal mountains, the Cascades, and the Sierra Nevada; the Great Basin on the east side of the Sierra and extending down through Inyo County; the Sonoran or desert province covering the Mojave and Colorado deserts; the California Island province off the coast; and finally the Californian province, that area most distinctly Californian, of chaparral and oak savanna, mixed evergreen forest, marshlands and prairies, which occupied the greater part of the state. These biotic provinces and their subdivisions were even more clearly marked in the pre-European days than they are today. To some degree their divisions reflect the pattern of Indian occupancy, although this was not considered in drawing the provincial boundaries. The Oregonian province was the home of the Algonkian and Athabascan peoples; the Uto-Aztekans occupied the Great Basin and Sonoran provinces; the Penutians and Hokan dominated in the Californian province. But this separation does not hold up in detail, and it remains to be seen if any significant environmental preferences or adaptations were involved. Nevertheless, these provinces have provided the natural settings in which California history was to occur, and even today reflect different patterns of human use and occupancy. Intensive human settlement marked by city-scapes and farm-scapes is confined to the Californian province with its milder climates and richer soils. The other provinces, with sparse populations, remain tributary, supplying minerals, lumber, livestock, and water to the metropolitan areas or serving as recreation space for their people.

CHAPTER TWO

The Displacement of Wildlife

O F ALL THE ENVIRONMENTAL changes that have taken place in California, perhaps none had such an immediately obvious and dramatic effect as the decline in wildlife from abundance to scarcity. This resulted from the impact of European colonists and was to touch off one of the first conservation movements in California, a movement that is stronger today than heretofore.

The term *wildlife* in its present usage has an American origin. In theory it refers to all wild animal life. In practice it refers to the larger, more conspicuous or economically important vertebrate animals—with the exception of fish. Thus we have a federal Fish and Wildlife Service and a state Department of Fish and Game which have been traditionally concerned with economically important vertebrates. The following pages refer to wildlife in the sense of the larger, more conspicuous forms. since these are the ones for which there is a historical record.

Of California's six biotic provinces, two are almost exclusively in California (they extend into Baja California), and four are generally outside the state. This division means that California had not only its own unique fauna, but also representatives of the Great Basin, Sonoran, Oregonian, and Sierra-Cascade fauna. Furthermore, because of its climate and the originally great extent of marshes and inland waters, California is a major wintering ground of the waterfowl and other birds that come down the Pacific Flyway from breeding areas in Alaska and Canada. This diversity of fauna is not to be equaled elsewhere in America outside of the tropics.

Such diversity makes it almost meaningless to write about wildlife in general. To say that the wildlife of California has declined seriously in abundance is true, if we mean that California now supports a lesser biomass of wild animal life than it did at the time of European settlement. But in this general statement we lose sight of the fact that some species—like the raccoon, the mule deer, the ground squirrel, the mockingbird, Brewer's blackbird—are probably more abundant today than in the past, whereas others—like the grizzly, wolf, wolverine, and California condor—are extinct or near extinct. To illustrate this, a few species or groups of species will be considered in some detail.

Undoubtedly the most spectacular land animal to survive the post-Pleistocene extinctions in California was the grizzly bear (*Ursus arctos*). This bear was the same species, but a different race of the grizzly, that once occupied a large area of North America and Eurasia. The grizzly was sufficiently distinct in appearance to be considered a separate species when it was described by taxonomists. In fact, C. Hart Merriam, who first classified the grizzly, named seven different species in California on the basis of their skulls and teeth, of which the southern California type was considered the largest, with males weighing over 1400 pounds. Like top predators anywhere the grizzly was fearless, for it had nothing to fear. The Indians could kill a grizzly, but more often in an encounter the grizzly killed the Indian. Being large and bold, the grizzlies impressed early Europeans with their abundance.

Bears of great size, many bear tracks, and bear trails were reported all along the south coastal region that was visited by Spanish explorers, and particularly in the San Francisco Bay area. Considering their abundance, their frequent ferocity, and the ease with which they were seen, one would think that bears should be well described and well known, but in fact they are not. In their classic *Fur-Bearing Mammals of California*, Joseph Grinnell, Joseph Dixon, and Jean Linsdale commented:

It is a curious fact that the larger the animal the more difficulty we have found in gathering accurate information about it. Great numbers of people, pioneers or those living of later years in the less settled parts of the State, have been alert to seize any and every opportunity to *kill* bears. Their attitude has been adventurous, as a rule, or else founded on determination to destroy a marauder or a supposedly dangerous enemy. Barely has an effort been made to get more than the knowledge necessary to bring success in hunting; and even this knowledge, not set down in writing at the time, becomes blurred in the telling, so that the earnest seeker after facts usually finds himself baffled by obvious misstatement or at least exaggeration.[1]

Nevertheless, we have sufficient accounts of bears being in abundance. In Humboldt County Calvin Kinman recorded that he and his father counted forty bears in sight at once from a high point in the Mattole country. J. S. Newberry in 1857 also noted that bears "are rather unpleasantly abundant in many parts of the Coast Range and Sierra Nevada in California, where large numbers are annually killed by the hunters, and where not a few of the hunters are annually killed by the bears." Jedediah Smith in 1838 encountered grizzlies frequently as he traveled down the Sacramento River while trapping beaver, and he had little doubt that they were common throughout the Central Valley.[2]

In the Fort Tejon area, John Xantus found grizzlies to be in great abundance: "They are really a nuisance, you cannot walk out half a mile without meeting some of them, and as they just now have their cubs, they are extremely ferocious so I was already twice driven up a tree, and close by the Fort."[3] James Capen Adams, in the early 1850s, made his living capturing and selling bears and traveled around the state with two tame grizzlies he had captured and raised as cubs. By the 1860s, when William Brewer traveled through California, bears were still relatively common, but the decimation had long been under way and was having its effects.[4]

The last grizzly in Humboldt County was killed in 1868, in Mendocino in 1875, in Santa Cruz in 1886, in Monterey in 1886, in Los Angeles County in 1916. The last bear in captivity died in 1911. The last grizzly reported killed in California was in the Sierra Nevada in Tulare County in 1922. The last grizzly reported to be seen in the wild in California was in Sequoia National Park in 1925. They were big, they threatened, they ate livestock, and they killed people, and in consequence they were poisoned, shot, and exterminated.

By contrast the black bear has managed to survive. Perhaps because the species was not a top predator and lived with experience of grizzly bears, it was not particularly aggressive toward people. Few people, if any, have been killed by black bears, although many have been scared and some injured through taking undue liberties with semi-tame national park bears. The black bear belongs to the widespread American species *Euarctos americanus*, of which two separate races occur, one in the northern coast ranges and the other in the Sierra Nevada and Tehachapis. They average less than half the size of the grizzly, since the largest grizzly could weigh a ton, and black bears rarely exceed 500 pounds. They occupied the higher elevations of the mountains, above the chaparral and woodland belt where grizzlies were most numerous. They did not live in the south coast ranges or the mountains of southern California for reasons not easy to explain.

The black bear has not escaped the harassment to which all large predators are subjected, since it kills sheep and occasionally other livestock. Sheep owners still detest bears and kill them whenever possible, even though the species is given some protection by law and may be taken by sport hunters only in prescribed seasons and by specified methods. They have survived because they were wary and willing to hide and because protection came soon enough.

The large wild grazing animals of California, unlike the carnivores, in no way threatened man directly, but they occupied space he wanted to use. They were good to eat, their hides were useful, and their heads in the opinion of some people seemed suitable for adorning the walls of homes. Their abundance at the time of European arrival was noted by all who recorded the California wildlife scene.

The Spanish, traveling northward from San Diego, first encountered the tule elk in the vicinity of Monterey Bay and then found them in great abundance on the plains and hills surrounding San Francisco Bay. To the extent that they visited the Central Valley, they noted the presence of elk there also. Later visitors were more ecstatic about the great abundance of game in the Central Valley, where the tule elk was the most conspicuous species. This was the stronghold of the tule elk, which roamed throughout, feeding in the grasslands and the tule marshes. They roamed as far south as the Tehachapis and across the south Coast Range to the Salinas Valley and Monterey Bay. They were numerous around San Francisco Bay and northward to the Russian River. There they were replaced by the Roosevelt elk which occupied the forested mountains and river valleys northward into Oregon and Washington.

The onslaught against elk began with the Gold Rush and the market for meat in the mining camps. In some areas they were rapidly hunted into extinction. From tens of thousands they dwindled to a few survivors which were protected on the Miller and Lux ranch in the Buttonwillow area north of Bakersfield. These few elk and their descendants were to help write an interesting chapter in the history of wildlife restoration, since they are now being brought back to their original native range. The Roosevelt elk were equally hard hit and wiped out throughout most of their California range with a few surviving in the redwood-covered north coastal ranges of Humboldt and Del Norte counties. Some of their descendants were to reappear much later as the Prairie Creek herd in the Redwood National Park.

The pronghorn antelope was probably more numerous than the elk. This species occurred in suitable grassy areas throughout the Mojave region and along the coast of southern California. It extended up the Great Basin side of the Sierra and in the north followed the Great Basin sagebrush vegetation halfway across Siskiyou County. The pronghorn were perhaps most numerous in the Central Valley, but they ranged into the lowlands around San Francisco Bay and across the south coast ranges into the Salinas Valley, Monterey Bay area, and the Santa Barbara—San Luis Obispo coastal plain. In 1924 a census taken by the California Academy of Sciences indicated that there were only a thousand left, living in the northeastern sagebrush region and in Fresno and Los Angeles counties. By the 1920s they were further reduced and the last of the valley and southern California antelope were dead. The remnants in Modoc and Lassen counties were saved and later contributed to the recent story of wildlife recovery and restoration.

The bighorn sheep story is equally depressing. Once they were reasonably abundant through the mountains along the

Great Basin side of the state and into the Cascades. Another population occupied the high Sierra. A third was distributed across the deserts and into the Tehachapi Mountains. A fourth occupied the higher mountains of Riverside and San Diego counties. The northern lava beds populations were exterminated; the Sierra sheep were drastically reduced. The desert sheep and southern peninsula bighorn survived in small numbers. The causes of the decline are believed to be severe depletion of essential forage resulting from heavy and uncontrolled use by livestock, the transference of diseases and parasites from domestic livestock, the increase of human activity, including appropriation of water of desert springs, and, finally, poaching. The bighorn, like the antelope, have been brought back, in part. Many populations, however, still exist precariously even though legally protected from hunting.

By contrast, the last of the species of large wild grazing animals is a story of survival and success. The small deer of California, belonging to the mule deer (*Odocoileus hemionus*) species, are adaptable. In pre-European times they were not especially abundant, being clearly overshadowed by the elk and antelope. They were fairly numerous around the more settled areas, where the Indians kept the brush burned and the forests open. They are successional species not inclined to favor either dense forests, tall brush, or the open bunch-grass prairies. Cutting of the forests, burning of the brush, and overgrazing of the prairies and the Great Basin plains favored the deer. Despite heavy hunting, which continued well into the 1930s despite the existence of game laws, deer not only survived, but increased. In a 1950 survey, there were an estimated million deer in California. It was a conservative estimate. Subsequently there has been a decrease in some areas, but a species that can adapt as well to the suburbs as to the wilderness seems unlikely to face extinction. Their nearest counterpart in Europe, the roe deer, has continued to thrive under even worse circumstances.

Many people hold the mistaken belief that the boundaries of California end where the sea meets this land. The geological state of California extends seaward to where the continental slope encounters the abyssal plain of the Pacific Ocean. The edge of the continental shelf—flat land, more or less—is at varying distances from the present shore line. Much of this extensive area has been dry land at various times in the past, just as much of the present dry coastal zone has been under water in the past. These changes are associated with the tying up in the world's ice caps of various amounts of water and have nothing to do with the more major ups and downs associated with movements of the earth's crust. They are going on now, and what will be the general trend over the next century or more we do not know. We do know that sea level is a movable marker.

Just as great herds of elk and antelope moved across the plains of the Central Valley in pre-European days, so also did great herds of sea mammals travel above the plains of the continental shelf, moving up the slopes of the islands and occasionally down into the depths of the submarine canyons. The abundance and variety of these sea mammals were greater than those of their terrestrial counterparts. However, they included no grazing herbivores equivalent to deer or mountain sheep. Some fed on the floating plankton, some on the fish who fed on the plankton, and some on the mammals that fed on the fish that fed on the plankton. The largest of them all, the baleen whales, fed on the smallest planktonic prey.

Few people realize even today, with the current interest in whales, how many kinds of sea mammals occur in California waters. There are twenty-six species of cetaceans, the whales and dolphins, of which seven are the baleen whales, three are toothed sperm whales, three are beaked whales, also with teeth, and thirteen are in the dolphin-porpoise group which includes the killer whale. There are seven species of seals and sea lions, and one sea-going otter. It is impossible to know the relative abundance of these species in Indian times, since the existence of many was not known. The sea-going Chumash were most familiar with them—dolphins played a role in their religion, and the killer whale, represented in remarkable soapstone carvings, was apparently regarded as a friendly being—he is shown smiling. Sea otters provided skins for clothing and trade. Seals and sea lions were food sources. Sea mammals were apparently abundant and were easy prey later to those who had dollar signs in their eyes and slaughtered them for profit.

Even around Monterey Bay, the Ohlone Indians, who were

not sea-farers, received a high percentage of their animal protein from sea mammals. One may assume also that if a whale washed ashore anywhere within sight of people, it would be eaten. The Canalino peoples used whale carcasses for the structural supports of their houses. A hundred-foot-long blue whale could shelter a lot of people. The abundance of whales in Monterey Bay caused one observer to complain about both their familiarity and the "nauseating odor" they give off when breathing.[5]

The most abundant species among the larger whales originally included the right whale, which migrated to and from Arctic waters in the spring and fall. It is now severely endangered. The humpback whale may have used Monterey Bay as a breeding area, similar to what is now found in Hawaiian waters. Summers were spent in the Arctic. Grey whales did not remain in California but passed through its waters from December to February on their way to breed in Scammon's Lagoon (Ojo de Liebre) in Baja California, or in other bays along the coast of Mexico. In March and April they moved north again along the coast of California. These are still the whale-watcher's whale, easily visible from shore as they swim through the Santa Barbara and San Pedro channels and along the San Diego coast. They too spend the summer in Arctic waters feeding on the abundant plankton. The fin whale, one of the largest whales, was abundant off the coast in the summertime and is still the most likely whale to be seen in summer. The sperm whale was reasonably numerous, but like the fin, less likely to be close to the shore. Three other species, the blue whale, largest of them all; the sei whale; and the small minke whale (up to 33 feet long) were present, probably in lesser numbers.

News of the abundance of whales in California had reached New England by the end of the eighteenth century. In the early 1800s, New Bedford whaling ships were in California waters pursuing the right and sperm whales—the former for whalebone and the latter for its oil. In 1851 shore-based whaling began in California, using small boats which could operate near shore and haul the whales to shore stations. These whalers concentrated on the humpback and later the grey whale. By 1875, the *Handbook to Monterey and Vicinity* stated that

The whale fishery, which for the last twenty-five years has constituted one of the most important of our local industries, is likely soon to become a thing of the past. The whales are gradually becoming scarcer. . . . Many years ago . . . the New Bedford whaling ships caught large numbers of Sperm and Right whales along this coast; but these species have now almost disappeared, and our whalers have to content themselves with the more numerous but less valuable California Greys and Humpbacks.[6]

The greys and humpbacks were soon to join the right and the blue whales on the endangered species list. Still, whaling continued intermittently in California. Shore stations in San Francisco Bay opened as late as the middle 1950s, with killer boats operating off the coast. During their years of activity, until all American whaling was stopped by federal legislation in 1970, they killed: 1054 fins, 841 humpbacks, 379 seis, 783 sperms, 317 greys, 48 blues, and 21 smaller whales, along the continental shelf and slope from Point Arena to the Golden Gate.[7]

The grey whale had been given international protection in 1938 (though shore stations continued to kill them). This protection proved effective and their numbers increased to 12,000. It was estimated that there were once 30,000, but this is a guess. The blue, humpback, fin, and sei are considered threatened species. The sperm is still present but in reduced numbers. Maybe they will recover, though it will be a long time before they crowd the boats in Monterey Bay and the pollution from their bad breath takes the place of petroleum fumes in the Monterey air.

The smallest of the marine mammals, the sea otter, received an inordinate amount of unwelcome attention because of its coat, reckoned to be among the finest of furs ever to be used as an adornment of the human frame. In Indian times otters and one of their principal food items, the abalone, were equally abundant along the California coast. The otters were not only abundant, but tame, coming out on shore to rest after a hard day of diving for shellfish. The Indians killed otters from time to time, but had little effect on their numbers or their attitudes. Otters once ranged from Japan to the Aleutian chain and thence down the Pacific Coast to Baja California. They are usually divided into two subspecies, the northern, based in Alaska, and the southern, from the Farallones south to Baja California and with high populations around the California islands.

In 1740 a Russian navigator, Vitus Bering, along with a German naturalist, Wilhelm Steller, undertook a voyage of exploration into the Aleutians. They brought back hundreds of sea otter skins and started a market for these furs. Pursuit of the sea otter, soon after accompanied by its elimination, led the Russians down the Pacific Coast of North America. In 1812, they established a base at Fort Ross in Sonoma County, and then moved southward to the Farallones and the southern California islands. Hunting was done by Aleuts from Alaska, who took time off from otter hunting to slaughter hundreds of the Channel Island Indians—a condition that contributed to the removal of the Indians from the islands to the mainland during the 1820s and 1830s. American and English ships joined in the trade, also with Aleut crews. George Nidever reported a pitched battle against the Aleuts on Santa Rosa Island in 1836, the first, he states, in which they were defeated. He went on to say, "Landing occasionally on the islands, they attacked the almost defenseless natives, killing many of them, as the piles of human bones on these islands, especially on that of San Nicolas, abundantly testify." [8]

The unchecked slaughter of sea otters, which lacked natural enemies and are slow breeders, led to their virtual disappearance from the North American coast. Some protection came in 1911 with the signing of a treaty among the governments of the United States, Russia, Japan, and Canada which protected fur seals and sea otters; and the passage of strict legislation by California in 1913. But by then the otters were very few—some in Alaska and perhaps a few dozen in California. In 1938 a large herd of otters had reestablished itself off the Monterey coast, and there were several other smaller groups further south. Since then they have come back considerably with perhaps more than two thousand off the Monterey–San Luis Obispo coast or in smaller groups reported from time to time from the Channel Islands to Humboldt County. Meanwhile, the Alaskan herds have made a strong comeback and transplants have been established off Oregon and Washington.

One would believe that the sea otters could now have a reasonably secure future. But there are still other perils to their safety. Abalone hunters, clam diggers, and other commercial and sport fishermen have started an anti-otter campaign—claiming that the little beasts are destroying the abalone fishery and encroaching on all shell fisheries. Their charges have limited merit. The ability of tens of thousands of sea otters to live in harmony with the abalone is documented well back into prehistory. The ability of the commercial fishermen to do the same has yet to be demonstrated.

Other examples could be cited documenting the decline of species from abundance to a low level, and then the subsequent recovery (for many species) to a safe, if not abundant, population level. But space does not permit this. It seems unlikely that the original levels of wildlife abundance will again be reached. It is also unlikely that the close relationship that once existed among people and animals can be restored except in places set aside from usual human use.

Some writers, such as Malcolm Margolin, have noted the change in behavior of animals, reporting that in Indian times:

> Foxes, which are now very secretive, were virtually underfoot. Mountain lions and bobcats were prominent and visible. Sea otters, which now spend their entire lives in the water, were then readily captured on land. The coyote, according to one visitor, was "so daring and dexterous, that it makes no scruple of entering human habitation in the night, and rarely fails to appropriate whatever happens to suit it."[9]

Captain Frederick Beechey, writing of Spanish California, stated that the animals seemed to have lost their fear and to have become familiar with man. Today that old trust is returning in areas where animals have long been protected. It brings its own problems as bears usurp garbage cans, raccoons chase house cats out of their own kitchens, and deer consume the summer supply of vegetables from the kitchen garden. One cannot have everything!

To review the story of wildlife, it is possible to document different periods in California wildlife history, and the same calendar fits well enough with other living resources. First were the thousands of years of relative harmony and balance between humankind and the natural world—Indian times. This was not because the Indians were necessarily nobler or better; rather it was primarily because their way of life did not reward those who took more than their share. No merit was to be gained, they felt, by the accumulation of wealth beyond a comfortable limit. They saw themselves as a part of nature—not as outsiders come to enrich themselves from it.

Indian times did not end with the Spanish, although the Indians were disrupted and decimated by disease in south coastal California. But the Spanish were not present in most of the state. Where they did live, their way of life, based on agriculture and pastoralism, provided them with an abundance. They did not become oriented toward slaughter or commercialization of wild animal life, perhaps because their jurisdiction ended before such activities became profitable.

The United States entered the California picture partly because the Russians had come in pursuit of the otter and seemed inclined to stay, partly because Americans desired trade and trapping, and finally because the discovery of gold brought people by the thousands from eastern America. With their coming, a period of wildlife slaughter and commercialization began which continued into the twentieth century. By the time it could be checked, some species were extinct or faced with extinction, and any that could be eaten and sold, or that interfered with human exploitation of the land and its resources, were drastically reduced in numbers.

This destruction led in the late nineteenth and early twentieth centuries to the conservation movement. The movement for wildlife conservation was one of the first conservation activities to get a start in California. As early as 1852, the state legislature had passed laws intended to protect some of the more heavily hit species, but these laws had little effect. In 1870, a state Fish Commission came into being with the responsibility to regulate and restore the depleted fisheries of California. In 1878 this agency became a Fish and Game Commission, the first in the nation, with responsibility for restoring terrestrial wildlife as well as fish. In 1907 it became necessary to buy a hunting license to hunt game, and in 1913 a fishing license was required. Some revenue was acquired, and a Fish and Game Department with wardens came into existence. The fight to protect wildlife was all uphill at that time. It was not until the 1930s that wildlife conservation became reasonably effective.

The period since World War II has been a different era from

the years preceding it. It has been one of marked public interest in and concern for wildlife—one that received still further impetus with the rise of the "ecology movement" in the 1960s. It has been marked by successful wildlife restoration. At the same time, with increased populations, industrialization, high technology, and high economic expectations, it has brought new dangers. These, revolving around the issue of pollution, will be the subject of a later chapter. Suffice it to say here that the full extent of danger to wildlife from the variety of physical and chemical by-products of today's economy cannot yet be fully evaluated.

CHAPTER THREE

The Rangelands

O F THE SIX THOUSAND species of vascular plants in California, nearly a thousand have been introduced from other parts of the world. Of the remaining five thousand, nearly thirty percent are endemics—a high percentage for any area, even for islands. Endemics are species that occur in one place and nowhere else except when deliberately moved by man. Why there are so many in California is a question without a single answer. The great variety of habitats and the relative isolation provided by the deserts and high mountains contribute to it. California has undoubtedly provided a refuge for species that were once more widespread, but have been reduced by severe climatic changes elsewhere—the coastal redwoods and Sierra big trees, for example. The relative isolation of California has contributed to the richness of the flora, but has also given to it a vulnerability which one usually associates with island species. In relative isolation from competitors or predators, many California species lacked the ability to compete successfully when more aggressive species were brought into the state. Many had not developed, or had lost, the adaptations needed for survival. This was true of those species that made up the original grasslands of California. If the buffalo or American bison had reached California, the grasslands over the years would have developed adaptations to the presence of a large grazing animal that traveled in great herds. The grassland would have been a different kind from that developed in the presence only of deer, elk, and pronghorn antelope, for these species of large animals did not prefer the tall perennials that made up the original California prairie.

Of all the families of flowering plants, grasses and grasslike plants (the sedges and rushes) attract the least interest. Everybody knows what grass is. Very few learn to identify the different kinds. A grass is a grass, except when it is growing in a lawn where most people learn to tell the species that they want to grow from the "weeds" that invade it. Livestock owners are an exception. Grasses are important to them, and they know how to differentiate the species. But this was not often true in the past. In consequence, few people realize that the grasslands of California have changed from what they were originally. This change has been one of the more sweeping alterations of the California environment.

To name the trees that grow in California is to bring to most readers some flashes of recognition. A redwood is different from a pine, from a maple, and from an oak. To name the grasses is to lose your audience, so the list will be kept at a minimum. All of the grasses of California, unlike those of the Midwest and East, are adapted to summer drought. Their growing season is relatively short. The hills green up and initial growth starts after the first rains of the autumn. As the cooler temperatures of winter set in, grasses become semidormant. When temperatures warm in the spring, usually March or April in the lowlands, rapid growth begins. Within a period of two or three months all growth is complete and seed heads are formed. Annuals then die back. Perennials enter a period of summer dormancy.

Perennial grasses dominated in the original California flora. They were of two principal forms: bunch grasses which grow upright in dense tufts of stems from a perennial root crown, and sod-forming grasses which spread out horizontally from underground or aboveground rhizomes or stolons. These latter are the preferred lawn grasses since they form a continuous cover over the soil—Kentucky blue grass and Bermuda grass are among the more common species. Bunch grasses were represented in the original California flora by the purple needle grass (*Stipa pulchra*), squirrel-tail grass (*Sitanion*), and the wheatgrasses (*Agropyron*) along with many others. The sod-formers included the salt-grasses (*Distichlis*) which grow in alkaline or saline areas, or the galleta grass (*Hilaria*) of the desert regions. Perennial grasses may grow for many years, the older portions dying back, but new shoots growing up. Perennial grasses may live to be very old. Annuals, by contrast, pop up each year from seed, go through their whole life cycle in a few months, form new seed, then die. There were many native annual grasses in California, but they were subordinate to the perennials, occupying disturbed areas or areas of thin soil for the most part or desert areas where the annual rainfall was insufficient to support an established grass cover.

The Spanish who first came to California brought livestock with them—horses and burros, cattle, sheep, goats, and swine. These animals found conditions to their liking. They increased and multiplied. Some were kept near the missions, or later on the ranchos, but others escaped and ran wild. Horses, cattle, burros, and goats adapted to life in the wild. By the time the American settlers came to California, herds of wild cattle and horses were even more common than elk and antelope in the Central Valley. The wild burros did particularly well in the deserts and sagebrush lands. Goats thrived especially on the Channel Islands where there were no predators. Domestic sheep did not adapt well to a feral life. Coyotes in California helped see to that. Initially the livestock business in California was based on cattle more than other species. A trade developed in hides and tallow, and this commerce became increasingly important until California's conquest by the United States.

The original grasslands were productive and the grasses evidently were of great nutritional value. Edwin Bryant, who came here in 1846, had the following comments:

> The horned cattle of California which I have thus far seen, are the largest and the handsomest in shape which I ever saw. There is certainly no breed in the United States equalling them in size. They, as well as the horses, subsist entirely on the indigenous grasses, at all the seasons of the year; and such are the nutritious qualities of the herbage, that the former are always in condition for slaughtering, and the latter have as much flesh upon them as is desirable.... The varieties of grass are very numerous, and nearly all of them are heavily seeded when ripe, and are equal if not superior, as food for animals, to corn and oats.[1]

These comments were written at a ranch near Mount Diablo. As Bryant traveled into the San Francisco Bay area he noted: "From this plain we entered a hilly country [near Livermore], covered to the summits of the elevations with wild oats and tufts or bunches of a species of grass, which remains green through the whole season."[2] In Santa Clara County he traveled "over a level and highly fertile plain, producing a variety of indigenous grasses, among which I noticed several species of clover and mustard, large tracts of which we rode through, the stalks varying from six to ten feet in height."[3]

Already, by Bryant's time, the changes had begun. The native grasses were still in place and "green through the whole season," but invaders, wild oats and mustard, were taking over.

The Spanish brought livestock, but they also brought food for their animals. In the hay, no doubt, were the seeds of many of the grasses and broad-leaved herbs (forbs) from the Mediterranean region of Europe. These were hardy plants, adapted already to the summer-dry, Mediterranean climate of California, but adapted also to thousands of years of heavy pressure from grazing livestock. They were the Eurasian survivors of ten thousand years of pastoralism. In California, wherever there was bare ground, they took hold. The invaders did not arrive all at once, or did not spread at the same time. The ones that moved out first required better soil and moisture conditions. These included species like the wild oat (*Avena*) and soft chess (*Bromus*), which are now rated among the better annual forage grasses. More hardy species of lower forage quality spread later, such as foxtail fescue (*Festuca*) and nitgrass (*Gastridium*). As conditions continued to deteriorate, grasses such as red brome (*Bromus rubens*) and cheatgrass (*Bromus tectorum*) took over large areas. The more recent invaders, Medusa-head wild-rye (*Elymus caput-medusae*) and goat grass (*Aegilops*) are good for little except to hold the soil in place, and not much good for that.

By the time that the first plant ecologists explored California, the grasslands had changed beyond recognition. Only by careful detective work, looking over areas that had long been protected from grazing—railroad right-of-ways, graveyards, or areas that for one reason or another had been fenced and protected— could the original flora be found. One worker, George Hendry, took the trouble to examine the straw from which the adobe bricks of the Spanish missions had been made. By working from the first missions to those last constructed, he was able to determine the sequence in which the introduced species became established and spread.[4]

It was the heavy grazing and trampling that contributed most to the change. Aggravating this situation were the periodic droughts that have always been a factor in the California environment. Severe droughts occurred in the early 1800s and brought serious livestock losses. Not only did the animals die, but before they died they pounded into dust the vegetation near the sources of water. In a dry year plant growth is necessarily limited, and plants become vulnerable to overgrazing. Livestock populations that had built up to high numbers during above-average rainfall years, when forage growth was luxuriant, remained alive to devastate ranges when the rains failed to come. Drought periods differed from one part of the state to another. Humboldt and Del Norte counties might well have an excess of rain while the rest of the state is parched. Southern California is often out of phase with northern California.

The drought of the 1860s was of unusual severity. William Brewer was traveling through California at that time and noted massive livestock losses and commented on the complete lack of vegetation in areas that would normally be grass-covered. Faced with total collapse, livestock owners took their animals into the mountains and even into the Mojave, where there was some forage to be found. George Nidever, who was then living on San Miguel Island, reported that in 1862 he had 6,000 sheep, 200 cattle, 100 hogs, and 32 horses on the island. In 1863 to 1864, he lost 5,000 sheep, 180 cattle, a few hogs, and 30 horses. In 1870 he sold out.[5] As a result of such experiences, San Miguel lost soil and vegetation and became for a time virtually a desert island. However, there have been worse droughts, and there will be again. The drought of the 1970s, which frightened most Californians into conserving water, seemed unusually severe because of the stresses now being placed upon the state's water resources, resulting from increased population, increased demand, and wasteful water use. Had it lasted as long as the dry years from 1897 to 1930, California's modern and wasteful economy could have faced drastic restructuring.

The 1860s put an end to the cattle boom in California and caused livestock owners to shift to sheep, which require less water and are more easily moved to available water and forage supplies. This set in motion a pattern of transhumance, or migratory sheep grazing, which virtually devastated the southern Sierra Nevada up to its highest meadows.

The first great trail herds of sheep began their long treks through the Sierra. For a time the unexploited mountain grasslands and meadows supported these animals, but as the ranges became overgrazed, carrying capacity decreased rapidly.

According to Roswell Welch of Porterville, a party traveling from Kernville to Mount Whitney in the 1890s found the land completely devastated by overgrazing by sheep. Most of the southern Sierra was in the path of the trail herds that used to leave southern Kern County and move over Breckenridge Mountain or around it, through the Walker or Olancha Pass area in Inyo County, thence up the east side of the Sierra, across Sonora Pass, and back via the west slope of the mountains to Kern County.

The establishment of the national forests and national parks, starting in 1890 to 1891, marked the beginning of the end of excessive exploitation of the high mountain ranges in California, but may also have had the effect of forcing greater pressure on the lowlands. The next drought period, beginning in 1890 in southern California and in 1897 farther north, had further effects. There was a gradual decrease of sheep at this time (from a high of six million in 1876) and a shifting of herds from California to the intermountain states. Nevertheless, in 1920 there were still nearly three million sheep in California and the numbers have not declined since.

In a document published in 1936, the Forest Service stated the results of its surveys and evaluation of rangeland conditions in the western United States. Some of the conclusions were shocking:

> Forage depletion for the entire range area averages more than half; the result of a few decades of livestock grazing.
>
> Three-fourths of the entire range area has declined during the last 30 years, and only 16 percent has improved.
>
> Probably not much over 5 percent of the entire range area is in a thoroughly satisfactory condition.

About seven-tenths, or 523 million acres, of the range area is still subject to practically unrestricted grazing.[6]

L. T. Burcham's studies of California in the 1950s essentially confirmed the Forest Service's findings. Not only had the carrying capacity declined by half so that it now took twice as many acres to support a cow or a sheep, but it was virtually impossible to maintain cattle on the range throughout the year without drastic decline in their condition and great danger of loss. The practice of livestock grazing has changed, with much greater reliance on irrigated pasture and feed lot, and much less pressure on the rangelands.

The degree of damage done to the rangelands differs from one part of the state to another. Recovery has been better in the higher rainfall areas and virtually nonexistent in the driest areas. The vegetation of the valley and foothill ranges has been changed permanently. Even with complete protection from grazing, or any system of grazing management short of replanting, the grasslands do not recover to the perennial grass cover of the past, but remain in annual grass cover. The invading grasses from Europe, like their human counterparts, are here to stay. Or so it seems at this time.

CHAPTER FOUR

Forests—
The Tallest,
The Biggest,
The Oldest

PEOPLE WHO LIVE in less favored parts of the world are often annoyed by being reminded of California's superlative qualities. But the truth must be stated. More of California was covered with forest and woodlands than with any other kind of vegetation. It still is, and this situation is quite remarkable when one considers the fate of forests in most lands with a similar Mediterranean climate. The forests of California are unusual in many respects. Not only do they include the world's tallest trees in the coastal redwoods (*Sequoia sempervirens*) of Humboldt County; the world's biggest trees in volume, the massive giant sequoias (*Sequoiadendron giganteum*) of the southern Sierra; and the world's oldest trees, the bristlecone pines (*Pinus aristata*), but also a greater variety of woody plants than is to be found in any region outside of the tropics.

The ancient redwood forests of California seldom fail to inspire awe in those who visit them for the first time. The term "cathedral groves" applied to their stands reflects the religious veneration in which they are held by many people. They are the last of a kind of forest that was once widespread in western America—you can find fossil redwoods in the hottest, driest desert regions. They survived in mild climate of the California coast with its abundant winter rain and summer fog. Redwoods are old—up to 2200 years. The tallest is measured at 367 feet, but rumor has it that there were taller ones that the loggers took down. In a favorable habitat they can live almost forever since they sprout from stump or root crown when they are cut down or burned. From southern Oregon southward to the last wind-shaped trees in the canyons of the Santa Lucias, they occupy the more sheltered and moist sites along the coast. Once there were almost two million acres of old growth, ancient redwoods. Most of that acreage came into private ownership, and the old trees were often cut down. Most that are left are in state and national parks. But the forests that were cut down, for the most part, grew back, and these second-growth forests themselves are impressive.

The giant sequoia of the Sierra was not as widely distributed as the redwood. Its remnant groves were found isolated along the western slopes of the Sierra from southern Placer County to Sequoia National Park. These trees were tall enough, up to 300 feet, but their massive quality distinguishes them since they have diameters up to 37 feet. The loggers had a crack at them also, but found that the trees tend to shatter when they hit the ground. Some groves were cut over, but most were protected when the national parks of the Sierra were established. The oldest of the big trees started to grow back in the days when the Assyrians were conquering Babylon and have kept on through all the vicissitudes of Western Civilization. They were called the oldest trees on earth until somebody bothered to check the age of the twisted pine trees, the bristlecones that grow in one of the most unfavorable environments on earth—the White Mountains of eastern Mono County. In Elna Bakker's words: "At 11,400 feet, on a rain-shadowed range receiving roughly twelve inches of annual precipitation, hammered by gale-force winds sweeping unhindered over the high plateaus, with a growing season measured in weeks and substrates that vary widely in their fertility, it is amazing that trees are here at all." [1] But the oldest bristlecone pines have been growing right there through climatic changes from dry to wet and hot to cold since the earliest days of human civilization in the Middle East.

To end with the superlatives, the sequoias and bristlecones are representatives of the conifers—the cone-bearing, needle-leaved, softwood trees—of which California has the greatest diversity: 24 species of pines alone, 54 species of all conifers, and 21 endemic species of conifers. In broad-leaved, deciduous trees, California cannot compare with the eastern forests, but it has a great variety of broadleaf trees, including 16 species of oaks, the providers of the staple foods of the California Indians.

The Indians did not make much use of the tall forests, but they affected them through their use of fire. The extent of this effect has been the subject of argument between those who regard fire as an enemy of forests (the Smokey-the-Bear people) and those who regard fire as an essential factor in forest management (the burners). The evidence now favors those who believe that Indian burning was important. From the earliest Spanish explorers, we have accounts of fires burning along the California coast. From the first Spanish settlements, there is evidence of concern about widespread burning by Indians, since the Spanish had buildings and livestock to protect. In 1793, at Santa Barbara, Governor José de Arrillaga made the following proclamation:

> With attention to the widespread damage which results to the public from the burning of the fields, customary up to now among both Christian and Gentile Indians in this country, whose childishness has been unduly tolerated, and as a consequence of various complaints that I have had of such abuse, I see myself required to have the foresight to prohibit for the future (availing myself if it be necessary, of the rigors of the law) all kinds of burning, not only in the vicinity of the towns but even at the most remote distances. . . .[2]

Thus began a series of regulations and laws, enacted many times in California, intended to prevent forest and range fires. One cannot say that these laws were to no avail, only that their effectiveness has not been what the lawmakers hoped for.

Concerning the effects of Indian burning and naturally caused lightning fires in the Sierra Nevada forests, Harold Biswell of the University of California has this to say:

> Ponderosa pine-grasslands are dependent on frequent surface fires for their health and stability, and on the other hand, frequent

surface fires are dependent on the plant community that produces the fuels that carry fire, each being dependent on the other. . . . I think that naturally occurring and Indian set fires must have burned portions of about every section of land of ponderosa pine forests in the Sierra Nevada each summer. Based on this analysis, the Sierra Nevada pine forests could easily have burned every 2 or 4 years on the average with many spots burning every year for 2, 3 or more years in succession.[3]

Not only the ponderosa pine forests were fire dependent. The same was also true of the Monterey pine, bishop pine, knobcone pine, and lodgepole pine forests (the closed-cone pines) since most of these require fire to open their cones and permit the seeds to germinate. The role of fire in the giant sequoias has also been extensively investigated. Frequent burning by Indians and by lightning kept the forests open. The light fires burning in sparse fuel at the ground surface did not develop into the forest-destroying crown fires that later became the rule. The coastal redwoods also have a fire history. Not only are the trees themselves extremely fire-resistant, but their seedlings survive best in areas cleared of litter and debris by fire, disturbance, or other factors. Other than their efforts to stop Indian burning, the Spanish and Mexicans themselves did not have major effects upon forests. Their style of building, based on adobe and tile, made few demands upon the available timber supply. They did use beams of oak, pine, or redwood, but their equipment for felling trees was limited. The Russians, much more timber-oriented than the Spanish, took steps to establish a California timber industry. According to A. Duhaut-Cilly, who visited Fort Ross in 1827:

> We went with M. Shelikof to see his felling of wood. Independently of the needs of the establishment, he cuts a great quantity of boards, small beams, thick planks, etc., which he sells in California, the Sandwich Islands and elsewhere: he has entire houses built which may then be transported taken apart. The trees he cuts are almost all firs of various species and in particular one called *palo colorado*. . . . It is the largest tree I have ever seen.[4]

As Americans drifted into Mexican California, many of them turned to logging, often on lands such as those around Santa Cruz where they had no legal right to be. The first mechanical sawmill in California may have been established by Joseph Chapman in 1822. The first commercial, water-powered mill was built by John Cooper just off the Russian River in 1834. It was washed away in the wet winter of 1840–1841. As early as 1839, the Mexicans became concerned with the effects of logging by foreigners:

> In 1839, Minister of Interior Romero of Mexico issued a paper in which he pointed out the evil results of repeated droughts. Harvests had failed and cattle had died. Said he, tradition and experience indicate that devastation of the forests and denudation of hills and mountains are influential causes of drought. Therefore, said Romero, cutting of forests should be restricted, replanting of trees should begin.[5]

The same correlation was to be made repeatedly in California along with the accompanying efforts to restrict cutting. Not much success can be noted.

With the gold rush and California's entry into the Union, the demand for timber and the rate of cutting accelerated. Readily accessible timber near the population centers was fast disappearing, as was noted in the *California Daily Chronicle* of San Francisco in 1854:

> Soon the whole neighborhood will be cleared of growing timber. Already the fairest and largest trees have fallen before fire, axe and saw. Those magnificent pillars which form so strange a crown to the mountains, when seen from San Francisco and the bay, are slowly disappearing.[6]

In most of the state, however, the feeling prevailed that the timber was "inexhaustible," and the biggest concern of the inhabitants was how to get hold of it. With the entrance of California into the Union, all except 9 million acres of land, recognized as private land, became public domain. Some of it was given to the state in support of education (two sections in each township) and another large area to the railroad companies as encouragement for developing a transcontinental route. Some of it was available in 160-acre pieces under the Homestead Act of 1862. However, timber was being raided in many areas. In 1862 there were 167 steam sawmills and 162 water-power mills busily cutting 166 million feet of timber and 28 million shingles.

Concern was expressed, particularly by the state's growing agricultural community, that more effective protection be provided for the forests and watersheds of California in order that the effects of flooding and the consequent deposition of silt and debris be ameliorated. The widespread cutting of forests was deplored, and an even greater concern was expressed concerning the forest and brush fires, many of which started in the slash and fallen trees left behind on cut-over lands. As early as 1850, a state surveyor-general was appointed and charged with such tasks as making plans for "planting, preservation, and increase of forests and timber trees." He was not given the means to accomplish this task.

By 1872 forest destruction had been going on with little check in many areas of the state. It was a common practice for cattle and sheep men to set fire to the forest when leaving the high mountain ranges at the end of the summer grazing season in order to improve the grazing for the next year. Whether such fires were or were not harmful to the forests depended on the dryness of the vegetation at the time it was burned and the amounts of fuel available. When it was hot and dry, and where fuel was plentiful, forests were destroyed and watersheds left without cover. In 1872 the state legislature made still another effort to prevent fires with a bill establishing stiff penalties for setting fires on state or federal land.

In 1881 the state legislature passed a concurrent resolution noting that "the forests in this State are being rapidly destroyed by reckless and wasteful cutting . . . [and] by the ravages of goats and sheep," and called on the federal government to take steps to preserve the forests. In 1885 the first state Board of Forestry was created and soon became involved in pressuring the federal government to do something to protect the forests of the public domain.

Meanwhile, two activities had been going on in the state which were not directly concerned with forests and forestry, but were having adverse effects. The first of these concerned the gold fields where, starting in the 1850s, miners were shifting from placer mining based on panning, sluices, and rockers to hydraulic mining, in which streams of water were directed at hillsides to wash away gravel deposits and soil in order to get at gold which had been laid down in ancient stream beds. This practice washed away whole mountainsides, trees and all, and created enormous destruction. Severe floods which almost wiped out Sacramento in the 1860s were associated with this practice, since stream beds were choked with debris from the gold fields. Nevertheless, by 1876, more than 100 million dollars had been invested in hydraulic equipment, and great areas were being affected. In 1884, agricultural interests in the Central Valley won a court battle against the miners which was the beginning of the end of hydraulic mining.

Perhaps more pervasive than mining was the activity of the grazing interests which were permitted to run their cattle and sheep without check on rangelands, both public and private. This caused particular concern to private landowners who were required to fence their lands in order to protect them, and even then found too often that their fences had been cut to allow migratory herds to be moved through. A law passed in 1871 was intended to prevent this evil and afforded another legal device for protecting forested areas from the harmful effects of excessive grazing.

The long-awaited action by the federal government to protect the public domain finally began toward the end of the nineteenth century, after fifty years of neglect. The creation of Yellowstone National Park in Wyoming in 1872 had established a precedent by which the federal government might set aside and protect parts of the public domain as future recreation areas for people and also for protection of nature. This precedent was followed by setting aside Yosemite and Sequoia reserves in the Sierra Nevada, along with the General Grant section of giant sequoias, as national parks. The next year Congress made it possible for the president to set aside additional areas, the forest reserves, which were in 1905 to become the national forests. The first in California and the second in the nation was the San Gabriel Forest Reserve of 500,000 acres established in 1892, followed by the Sierra Forest Reserve of 4 million acres, and the San Bernardino and Trabuco reserves of 800,000 acres in 1893. By 1905 nearly 86 million acres were included in the national forest system.

With the establishment of national parks, under the Department of the Interior, and national forests—after 1905 in the Department of Agriculture—some degree of control and management over the forested areas of California became possible. Control of grazing was one activity that was immediately undertaken. Grazing was not permitted in the national parks and was

restricted seasonally and by number and class of livestock in the
national forests. This control was sufficiently effective for some
recovery of the overgrazed mountain grasslands to take place
Control of forest fires soon took over as a first priority for
protection of the national forests. It became almost dogma with
the Forest Service that fire was bad and had to be prevented
from happening, anywhere, anytime. The result of this policy,
inevitably, was fuel accumulation and the growth of brush and
young trees under the canopy of the old forest. This almost
guaranteed that when fires started and got away, they would
become highly destructive. An earlier recognition of the value
of prescribed burning, carefully controlled at times when escape
of the flames was unlikely to occur, might have spared the
forests from future trouble. But it was not until research carried
out by the University of California at Berkeley in the 1940s and
1950s established the value of controlled fires that the anti-
burning policy began to change.

The purposes for which the national forests were set aside
were spelled out in the Forest Management Act passed by Congress in 1897: "to improve and protect the forests, aid in water
flow, and to furnish timber." Their use was to provide a per-
petual, sustainable yield of all products of economic value. In
fact, in their early years, there was little demand for national
forest timber since many of the more productive timber stands
had already come under private ownership. Especially in the
forests of the redwood region was there little reserved land of
any kind. The cutting of redwoods, which began near Monterey
and San Francisco, spread north through Sonoma and Mendocino counties. A new center for the redwood industry came into
being around Humboldt Bay, working into the giant stands of
Humboldt and Del Norte counties. Despite a strong public
demand for protection of the redwoods, not until 1901 was the
first of the California redwood state parks, Big Basin in the
Santa Cruz mountains, established. Some idea of the rate at
which timber cutting had increased in California is given in the
table on the facing page.

Until the end of World War II most timber cutting was done
on private lands, but the supply could not meet the demand as
old-growth stands of private timber were depleted. The Forest
Service came to the rescue by selling additional timber to pri-

Year	Estimated board feet of timber cut
1849	20,000,000
1869	318,817,000
1899	737,035,000
1923	2,118,094,000
1943	2,353,000,000

vate companies as well as by providing access roads to areas that had formerly been considered too remote for harvesting. Over the years many felt the Forest Service had entered too whole-heartedly into the timber-supplying business at the expense of other resources of public interest and value. In 1977, approximately 4.8 billion board feet of timber were harvested in California. Of that total, 1.7 billion board feet were harvested on National Forest land. A citizens' committee report, prepared for the Secretary of Resources and the governor of California, stated in 1979: "The deleterious effect which the present level of timber harvest is having on other forest resources cautions against consideration of an increase in the level of harvest until present adverse effects are corrected."[6]

Although the cutting of timber and even the damage from devastating forest fires do not generally result in the replacement of forest cover by other vegetation types, there are circumstances under which they do. Extensive hot wildfires can destroy an area too large to be reseeded naturally from those trees that have survived in outside unburned areas. The lower edges of forest in the Sierra and coastal mountains have been pushed upward over the years, and chaparral has taken over on formerly forested lands. On the dry, desert side of the Sierra and on the southern California mountains, forest fires can result in the replacement of trees by vegetation more tolerant of aridity. In some areas, logging and burning were deliberately used to replace forest with grassland and make room for live-stock grazing. Although this practice was discontinued when the value of forest products increased after World War II, it did result in extensive areas, particularly in the north coastal ranges, being changed over at least for some decades to grazing lands.

Logging carried on without regard for its adverse effects has undoubtedly contributed to flood damage. Although forest clearing in California does not affect the amount of rain that falls, the rate of runoff and erosion from cut-over lands exceeds that from forested lands and is even higher from burned-over areas. This results in siltation of stream beds, increased flood levels, and flood damage. In low rainfall periods, rapid runoff and decreased infiltration of water into the soil and water table can increase the severity of drought in the lowlands. Where silt and forest debris accumulate in stream beds, their ability to support fish decreases. This condition has been particularly evident in the coastal streams where salmon and steelhead trout once migrated from the ocean to spawn in great numbers. The commercial and sport fishery for salmon in California has been seriously affected, as has the sport fishery for steelhead.

California's mountains are still green with forests, which may be due to the resilience of nature rather than to human foresight. However, California has saved through its system of national and state parks, forest wilderness areas, and other reserves a creditable amount of its original, primeval forest for the benefit of future generations. The national forests and the privately owned timber lands are still vegetated with thriving second-growth forests over most of the land that was originally in forest cover. A small percentage of forest has been lost to urban development, transportation, agriculture, and pasture. A larger percentage has been lost for the time being to chaparral, grassland, or sagebrush vegetation, but most of that land can be reclaimed if reforestation is carried out. Damage that has been done to watersheds, wildlife habitat, fisheries, and recreational areas can be repaired with time and effort. Californians can afford some self-congratulation for what has been saved, but the road back to full recovery of forest productivity remains to be traveled.

CHAPTER FIVE

Water—
Too Little and
Too Much

THE HISTORY OF water development in California is marked by two truly impressive occurrences. One which happened long ago may well be the most spectacular single environmental blunder in history, the accidental creation of the state's largest inland water body, the Salton Sea. The other is still going on, but has already resulted in the world's largest water control and water movement system created by human effort. Some believe it may prove to be one of the world's greatest examples of environmental mismanagement, but this is a minority viewpoint.

One could argue that California's water problems result from the first European settlers coming in the wrong door—from Mexico to the driest part of the state. Had the Russians, for example, established permanent northern settlements, Eureka might be the Los Angeles of today, able to draw on the abundant water resources of the north coast. But that view would ignore the fact that the agriculture on which the wealth of the state has been based does best in the long growing seasons and warm weather of its drier regions. Most of California's water has gone for agricultural use and not to the cities and their industries. Although it is true that Los Angeles has done some of the most spectacular, long-distance water grabbing yet seen on earth, it has not been only to quench the thirst, water the lawns, or fill the swimming pools of its citizens, but also to irrigate its agricultural lands.

California has a climate marked by droughts and floods. Land and water management can exaggerate their effects, but does not determine them. They occurred in Indian times; they will persist into the foreseeable future. It has been stated that the drought of 1976–1977 was the most severe on record for the state as a whole. However, southern California was much less affected than the north and was able to forgo delivery of water from state aqueducts for use elsewhere. But there were many droughts in Spanish times. In 1795 crops failed in the Los Angeles area. Between 1821 and 1832 there was an extreme drought in southern California; however, not atypically, the year 1825, in the middle of the dry years, brought one of the most severe early floods. By 1829, there was no pasture for sheep—livestock losses and range damage went on together. The drought of the 1860s had characteristics similar to the earlier one. Dry years started in 1855 or 1856, but then in the winter of 1861–1862 occurred the worst flood in history, with a lake sixty miles across forming in the Sacramento Valley and the city of Sacramento being inundated. Serious flood damage occurred also in southern California. The sequence was to go on with the droughts of the 1890s and the 1920s. One searches in vain for a regular periodicity and hence a predictability. The movements of high pressure areas and air masses over the Pacific remain beyond prediction or control.

The ten years from 1945 to 1954 were unusually dry in southern California, with 1953 the driest year recorded by the Los Angeles Weather Bureau. However, the floods of 1955–1956 in California were beyond anything that had happened since the 1860s. Whole communities were washed away in northwestern California; elsewhere Marysville and Yuba City were severely damaged; Santa Cruz was hard hit. The winter of 1964–1965 did almost equal damage to the north coast, whereas that of 1968–1969 caused great problems in the San Joaquin Valley. This pattern of unpredictability has caused the state to undertake its monumental water works aimed at preventing floods in the wet years and providing irrigation water in the dry. The drought of 1976–1977 put it to the test. Had the drought lasted one year longer, it could well have failed the test.

Long before any human beings started manipulating California's water system, the landscape and waterscape changed greatly from periods of high rainfall to drought periods. During the wettest periods, the lakes in the Great Basin region of northern California—Lower Klamath Lake, Clear Lake, Goose Lake, the Warner Lakes, Honey Lake, and many others were full of water, with the northern ones contributing to the Klamath and Pit River systems. To the south, Mono Lake would expand in size, whereas Owens Lake would overflow down the Owens River to fill the salt flats of the Mojave Desert. In the Central Valley, the Kern, the Kings, the Kaweah, and Tule rivers would pour into Kern, Buena Vista, and Tulare lakes to form an inland sea. A great expanse of water would occupy the lower Sacramento Valley. Clear Lake in Lake County and Lake Tahoe in the Sierra, hemmed in by mountains, would spill their surplus waters down Cache Creek or the Truckee River. During the drought years, all this would change—the northeastern lakes and Owens Lake would go dry, and the San Joaquin Valley would become desert-like, whereas the northern rivers would flow down narrowed channels to make their impoverished contributions to the Pacific.

Water manipulation through the construction of dams and irrigation canals started with the missions. The first is credited to San Diego mission in 1810. The original pueblo of Los Angeles received its water from irrigation by damming the Los Angeles River. However, surface water was not reliable without more extensive engineering works, so many southern Californians turned to tapping the water table—fed at that time by an abundant input from the Sierra Madre. According to W. I. Hutchinson:

> By 1900 there were more than 10,000 wells in Southern California, of which some 1,500 were artesian wells. Windmills dotted the land. Within two decades the artesian flow had practically disappeared, and wells had to be driven deeper and deeper and equipped with powerful electric pumps to raise the water.[1]

The use of water to generate electric power in California followed not far behind Thomas Edison's invention of the carbon-filament electric light globe. In 1891 William Kerckhoff built the West's first successful hydroelectric plant on the San Gabriel River. In 1892 the city of Pomona established a small hydroplant in San Antonio Canyon and claimed the first long-distance transmission of electricity over wires. Redlands joined in 1893 with a 10,000-volt generating plant in Mill Creek supplying the city. Not long thereafter, people were carried by the Pacific Electric Railway to the beaches and the mountains across lands that were to become the Los Angeles metropolitan area. By then, however, water supply had become the most compelling issue in southern California.[2]

Its communities were often built from irrigation colonies, and future cities were developed on a base of this irrigation agriculture. These cities later tapped the water resources of the coastal mountains. The Big Bear River in the San Bernardino Mountains was dammed in 1884 to form Big Bear Lake, to be followed in the 1890s by Lake Arrowhead. The resources hardly met the needs of small cities, but Los Angeles with its steadily growing population and expanding agriculture had already looked elsewhere, specifically at the Owens Valley, far across the Mojave Desert and up the eastern flank of the Sierra Nevada.

Meanwhile, the strange adventures that were to build an unplanned-for, unexpected inland sea were going on. In 1896, an irrigation engineer, Charles Rockwood, and a reclamation specialist, George Chaffey, had looked at what was then called the Colorado Desert. They saw rich, fertile soils in the area later to be called the Imperial Valley and discovered a source of water flowing at a higher elevation in the Colorado River some sixty miles away. All that was needed was to punch a hole in the Colorado's banks and run the water into a dry river bed, the Alamo River. In the wetter days of the distant past that river had carried water from the Colorado into the Salton Sink, 241 feet below sea level and once an arm of the Gulf of California. With the promise of irrigation water, these speculators were able to sell the desert land and finance the operation. It reflects upon the attitudes of the times that the Rockwood and Chaffey California Development Company cut a canal from the Colorado into Mexico, connected with the Alamo River bed, led the water back into California, and diverted it into irrigation canals to wet the new farmlands of the Imperial Valley. No permission was asked, or obtained, from the United States, Arizona, Mexico, or anyone else. By 1902, some 100,000 acres were under irrigation. The federal government then decided to discourage the practice of river stealing and moved to close down the operation. Mexico, however, was willing to help the speculators. The development company moved its river tap to the Mexican side of the border in 1904 with the promise of delivering half the water to Mexico. The next year happened to be a heavy rainfall year in the Colorado basin. The flood-swollen river found the new Mexican canal waiting to receive its water and delivered virtually its entire flow, instead of the planned portion, down the Alamo River. By the end of the floods in 1905, California had its largest inland water body, already well-stocked with Colorado River fish. The river, however, kept on coming. The Southern Pacific Railway, whose tracks had crossed the Salton Sink, joined in a two-year effort to control the flood. After much exertion, the flow was regulated.[3] The Imperial Canal continued to take water into Mexico, but the All-American Canal, put in north of the border some years later, fed the Imperial Valley. The Imperial and Coachella valleys, south and north of the Salton Sea, became highly productive farm lands. But never before, and hopefully not again, has human effort accidentally established a major water body of this size. No evaluation of the total environmental impact can be made.

The story of Los Angeles's acquisition of Owens River water has often been told. Despite all opposition, including the sheer physical difficulties of building dams in the Owens Valley and an aqueduct across the Mojave, water from the eastern slope of the Sierra two hundred miles away was delivered to the reservoirs of the San Fernando Valley in 1913. Since even this supply was inadequate to meet the needs of agriculture and industry in coastal southern California, Los Angeles reached further to tap the Mono Lake watershed as well and then turned to the Colorado. In the Colorado River was water drawn from the mountains of six western states, from as far north as Wyoming, from the summits of the Colorado Rockies, from New Mexico, from the Wasatch and Uinta mountains of Utah, from Nevada's short desert streams, and from Arizona which poured the seasonal floods of the Gila into the muddy river. California contributed almost no water to the stream, but was the first to make major demands upon its supply.

In 1935 President Franklin D. Roosevelt dedicated Hoover Dam, which backed up what was then the largest manmade lake in the world over the Nevada and Arizona deserts. In 1941 Parker Dam was completed and water flowed into an aqueduct across the Mojave to reach Lake Mathews near Los Angeles. But even this water was not considered to be enough, and Los Angeles looked north of the Techachapis to the rivers of northern California. A principle of some sort had been established by this time which could be stated as "those with more money and more votes can take water from those with less money and fewer votes, and can get them to help pay for the transaction."

San Francisco was also searching for water. In 1901 the city decided that a good place for a dam and reservoir would be the Grand Canyon of the Tuolumne River, a hundred and more miles almost due east of San Francisco. The fact that this area was in the newly established Yosemite National Park did not trouble the water seekers. News of the projected dam brought the first real contest between conservationists and water seekers with John Muir and the Sierra Club leading the opposition. After twelve years of controversy, San Francisco won, and in 1913 work started on the dam. Another aqueduct took shape, and water from Hetch Hetchy filled the Crystal Springs Lakes perched conveniently on the San Andreas fault above San Francisco. Ironically, while the battle was going on, San Francisco was nearly wiped out by the earthquake and fire of 1906 and then rebuilt.

Inspired by the efforts of private developers and city fathers, the state of California in collaboration with the federal government began the most ambitious water project of all. The results of the Central Valley Project and the State Water Plan, while perhaps not visible from the moon, are still an engineering feat unequaled on earth. Virtually every major river in the state that drains into the Central Valley, and some which originally did not, are dammed and controlled. Their waters are used to generate electric power, and then moved around the state through canals and aqueducts to meet the water demands of agriculture and the urban-industrial complexes. A controlled flow is allowed to move into the delta of the Sacramento–San

Joaquin rivers and then to San Francisco Bay and the sea—enough to keep aquatic systems alive and provide for navigational needs. Some of the largest reservoirs on earth have resulted, starting with Shasta Lake, behind Shasta Dam on the Sacramento, 4,500,000 acre-feet; Lake Oroville on the Feather, 3,500,000 acre-feet; Clair Engle Lake on the Trinity, 2,500,000 acre-feet; San Luis Reservoir, west of Merced, 2,000,000 acre-feet; Don Pedro, on the Tuolumne, 2,000,000 acre-feet, and so on. A good share of the Trinity River, which once flowed west to join the Klamath, now is backed up and pumped through a tunnel into the Central Valley. In 1973 the unending thirst of southern California received its libation from the north when water from the Central Valley was pumped up over the Tehachapis into Castaic Lake and farther south to Lake Perris.

But the demand goes on. There are those who want to back up the Eel River and the Klamath and send them south. In 1980 the legislature passed and the governor signed a bill to build a peripheral canal to facilitate the movement of Sacramento and other northern rivers southward around the delta. Pressure is also on to build a big drain to take waters back out of the San Joaquin Valley, waters that are heavily saline and polluted after having been used to desalinate the soils and irrigate the crops of the region, and dump them into San Francisco Bay. Those who want to go on building can point to the jobs that are created, the power that is generated, and the new lands that are brought into agricultural production. The system supports in part an agricultural enterprise that brought in cash receipts of more than 10 billion dollars in 1978. California has become the richest and most productive agricultural state in the United States, supplying nearly half the fruits and vegetables consumed in America.

At the end of the 1977 drought, the California water supply system was in a critical state. Water storage in the state system of 143 reservoirs had been reduced to 39 percent of average, and some were virtually dry. Runoff from all of California's streams was less than a fourth of normal. Urban dwellers were asked to cut back severely their use of water, and they responded admirably, reducing consumption by more than a fifth throughout the state, and by more than 50 percent in Marin County. Agricultural users were favored, but deliveries were cut by 60 percent for those drawing from the State Water Project systems, and 75 percent for those using water from the federal Central Valley Project. Agricultural production in fact was only reduced by 8 percent, but this was because farmers turned to taking another serious overdraft from the already depleted ground water supplies. In the Central Valley ten thousand new wells were put in during the drought, drawing in some cases on underground reservoirs which had only filled during the Ice Ages. The ground water reservoirs underlying the Central Valley are said to have a storage capacity of 100 million acre-feet— more than three Lake Meads but less than one Lake Tahoe. In a normal rainfall year the extent of overdraft on ground water reservoirs in the Central Valley is 1.5 million acre-feet; this is in excess of the amount that can be expected to enter through infiltration.

During the 1976–1977 drought the water usage for a resident of Marin County was restricted to 45 gallons per day. The actual use was less. The national average water use in urban centers is 150 gallons per day. In drier areas of California, during the summer when water is needed for lawns and gardens, per capita use in urban areas may exceed 600 gallons per day. However, only a little more than 8 percent of California's delivered water goes to domestic, commercial, and institutional use. Great savings by individuals do little to help the overall problem. Agriculture uses 87 percent of available delivered water. If ten percent of the agricultural use could be cut, the savings would exceed the amount used normally in all the households of the state, including those amounts used for backyard food production. The finger is pointed at the farmers of the state. But who are these farmers? California's population in 1980, approximately 23 million, consisted of 14 million people living in the urbanized areas from Los Angeles to San Diego, 5 million in the urban counties around San Francisco Bay, and one million in the Sacramento area, leaving only 3 million distributed over the rest of the state. Of those 3 million, some 353,000 were employed on farms in 1978 at the peak of the harvest season. Hired workers on farms in that year totaled 167,100, which leaves the farmers and members of farm families working on the farm at 186,000 people.[4] These are the people who took in cash receipts of 10 billion dollars.

California is not a land of small farmers and family farms.

From the earliest days the state has been characterized by large individual or corporate holdings—the Spanish land grants first, later such agricultural empires as that held by Henry Miller and Charles Lux (500,000 acres), or the Kern County Land Company, or the even greater Southern Pacific holdings. The average farm size in California is somewhat over 400 acres, but many little farms balance the very big ones. In 1940 there were around 90,000 farms in California less than 50 acres in size. In the same year there were somewhat more than 5,000 farms that averaged 4,000 acres in size. Since then the big have grown bigger and the small farms have mostly been absorbed into larger units. California farming is for the most part agribusiness, the farm being part of a corporate unit which takes in many other enterprises. Agriculture not only uses 87 percent of the developed water in the state, it is also a major user of energy and of agricultural chemicals which in turn are a source of some severe pollution problems of the atmosphere, the soil, and the water. Approximately 10 million acres, or one-tenth of the state's land, is in use for farm crops, temporary pastures, or temporary fallow.

California's agriculture and water development for agriculture have had a more severe impact upon the California environment than any other activities. The impact of urban development, commercial-industrial development, and transportation is more obvious and locally severe, but only directly affects a much smaller area of the state.

The impact of California's water and agricultural development cannot be fully stated since there are unknown, long-term consequences. Some effects are immediate and obvious.

The state's wetlands have been largely destroyed and hence the habitat for millions of waterfowl and other users of the marshes and swamps has been reduced. The blocking of the larger rivers by dams has changed the fisheries of the state. Originally the salmon, steelhead, and other sea-run fish provided a naturally supported fishery of great value. Now cut off from their original spawning grounds, the fishery is reduced and depends to a great extent on artificial propagation from fish hatcheries. The value of the once-wild rivers of the state as recreational resources—perfectly obvious to some, apparently invisible to others—has been much reduced. Only the north coast rivers remain wild, and although given permanent "wild river" status by the state legislature, their future is uncertain, for such protection can be revoked. The rate of renewal of the state's ground water resources has been reduced through drainage of the wetlands and by drying up of the lakes as well as by changes in the watersheds through logging, grazing, and other uses. At the same time a heavy overdraft on existing ground water resources continues. Irrigation of dry lands in the San Joaquin Valley and elsewhere, without the necessary provisions for drainage, has led to salinization of the agricultural soils. The productivity of 400,000 acres in the San Joaquin Valley has been reduced by salinization and this situation is growing worse each year.

Irrigation agriculture based on a water system subsidized by public funds has encouraged the development of large-scale agribusiness, oriented toward immediate profit rather than long-term care of the land. This movement tends to be monocultural, dependent on heavy energy inputs (mostly from scarce petroleum), maximum use of farm machinery rather than human labor, and heavy use of chemical fertilizers, herbicides, and pesticides. The self-sustaining quality of agricultural soils, which naturally depend on the continuing activity of soil organisms as well as the continuing shielding and enriching influence of plant cover, declines, and the soils become increasingly dependent on external nutrient supplies. At the same time increased use of fertilizers no longer brings an equivalent increase in yields. Soil erosion remains a serious problem caused by water runoff during rainy periods and wind erosion during the dry season. At the end of the 1977 drought, dust storms in Kern County resembled those in the Middle West during the dust bowl years and caused millions of dollars of damage. According to the state Department of Conservation

> We are losing soils in almost every region of the State to water and wind erosion much more rapidly than they form by natural processes. The statewide average loss is estimated to be between 6 and 6½ tons per acre per year. This rate is roughly equivalent to the loss of one inch of soil every twenty-five years. Since topsoils range in thickness from several feet to only a few inches, the statewide soil loss rate can be expected to cause severe problems in many areas of California in the not-too-distant future.[5]

Throughout history only those lands that have received continued personal attention from the people who farmed them have remained productive. The California system that has developed—based on cheap fuel, subsidized water, and heavy chemical inputs—is in all probability not ecologically sustainable since the inputs only partially replace the natural soil-building and restoring processes for which they are substituted. Furthermore, the water capture and delivery system itself is by no means permanent. Many of the earlier dams and reservoirs built in the state have since filled in from silt eroded from the watersheds above and debris carried down by floods. All of the dams and reservoirs have limited life spans under the best of conditions even with erosion carefully controlled. The best of conditions are not to be found. We do not have a system built like the pyramids to last for thousands of years, but rather one that must be repaired, replaced, and rebuilt at increasing cost over centuries to come.

There are 1200 dams and reservoirs in California, and few of them have collapsed. The collapses, however, have been spectacular. The failure in 1928 of the Saint Francis Dam near Los Angeles killed as many people as the San Francisco earthquake. The Baldwin Hills Dam collapse near Culver City did 50 million dollars worth of property damage. The collapse of the Hell Hole Dam on the Rubicon caused flooding which was contained by the larger Folsom Dam downstream. Although no dams have yet been lost as a result of earthquakes, some have been damaged, and none has yet experienced an earthquake as severe as the San Francisco earthquake of 1906 or the Inyo earthquakes of the 1870s. Some of them will be put to this test.

The construction of big dams gives a dangerous illusion of safety against floods. Dams can ameliorate the effects of flooding and control heavy runoffs, but no dam is built to contain the really big floods that occur from time to time. Where dams encourage building on flood plains they can increase the risk to human life and property. Current minimum standards attempt to provide protection from a ten-year flood for agricultural areas, and from a hundred-year flood for urban areas. This means that they are built to contain floods estimated to have one chance in ten, or one in a hundred of occurring during any given year. These estimates are based on past flood frequency.

An overall evaluation of California's development and use of water leads to the conclusion that there could have been a better way to go. California has been a water-wasteful state, particularly in its agricultural sector. Water development has been influenced to a disturbing degree by large landholders who seek large returns on their investments. Much more could and should be done with less, but there is no way we can undo what has been done, except over a long period of time. These questions will be returned to in a later chapter.

CHAPTER SIX

Cities, Industries, and Pollution

A LTHOUGH THE MANIPULATION of California's water produced the most physically impressive of all environmental changes in California, most visitors to the state and most residents are little aware of these changes. What most people see is the spread of urbanization with its accompanying industries and networks of transportation. California supports metropolitan areas surrounding Los Angeles and San Francisco that are among the world's largest, spreading via freeway, railway, and airways to San Diego in the south and to Sacramento in the north. Other large urban centers are around Monterey Bay, Santa Barbara, Bakersfield, Fresno, and Stockton. These cities and their connecting links are where nearly ninety percent of the people are found. It is difficult to convince visitors that California is still wild and virtually empty, or that there are places where one can travel 200 miles in California, in as straight a line as one can manage, and not see a human habitation. The north and south Coast Ranges, the Sierra, Great Basin, and Mojave are still wild country.

The agricultural lands of the state contribute in a massive way to the pollution of air, water, and soil. But their contributions are far less visible than the smog which colors the air, the factory effluents which pollute the waters, the oil which is spilled along the coast, or less fearsome than the invisible threat of radio-active contamination from nuclear installations.

From the time of Juan Rodríguez Cabrillo to the day of Gaspar de Portolá, nearly 230 years, there was probably no growth in California's population. From Portolá's day until the Gold Rush there was probably a decline, as the original Indians died off in great numbers from introduced diseases. It took forty years, from 1850 to 1890, to add the first million people to California's population, less than twenty to add the second million, less than ten to add the third, and less than five to add the fourth. Between 1950 and 1970 a million people were added every two years. It was not that California's people had learned to breed like rabbits. Immigration contributed the greatest increase. Between 1951 and 1963 California's growth rate annually varied from 3.3 to 4.6 percent, but then declined to a low of 0.7 percent in 1972. Thereafter, it has increased to 1.9 percent in 1978. Natural increase, from the excess of births over deaths, added its greatest numbers in 1961, and then de-creased steadily to a low point in 1973 when only 130,000 addi-tional people were contributed through births. Even in 1978, when the total added was 178,000, the rate of increase from births was only 0.8 percent. Net immigration, however, reached a peak of 388,000 in 1957, and since then, with some fluctua-tions, declined to a temporary low of only 10,000 in 1972. Immigration now adds more to the population than births and is again approaching the levels of the 1950s. The reasons behind these changes are many and not always discernible. The results are more obvious.

Approximately 10 million acres of California's land are used for cropland or related purposes, while only 1.6 million acres are rated by the Soil Conservation Service as being of the best quality in soils, drainage, topography, and other factors. Since most people who came to California settled in urban areas—and for the most part urban areas are located on the best agricultural lands—the growth of California's population has been at the expense of California's best farming lands. By World War II nearly two million acres of agricultural land in California had been converted to urban-industrial or other nonagricultural uses. From 1952 to 1955 the Soil Conservation Service reported the loss of 60,000 acres per year of farming land converted to nonagricultural uses. During the period of most rapid population growth in the late 1950s and early 1960s the rate of conversion of agricultural land increased to 90,000 acres a year. By 1978 the rate had dropped but was still significant at 50,000 acres a year. It would appear that from 3.5 to 4 million acres of farming land have been converted to nonagricultural uses— suburban developments, highways and roadways, industrial, and commercial developments. In the San Francisco Bay area few of the once-extensive fruit orchards and truck gardens remain. In the Los Angeles basin citrus groves have given way to houses. It has been reported that when the farming lands of England were converted to suburbs, the rate of food production actually increased, so diligently did English householders cultivate their backyard vegetable gardens. Until recently, Californians have not been so oriented toward home food production, but a new trend in that direction is evident. It may be that not all of the 4 million acres will actually go out of production. However, the area paved over by the more than 163,000 miles of freeways, highways, and roads in the state is likely to be out of production for a long time.

The building of a city involves the most complete environmental transformation that could result from any change in land use other than complete flooding or creation of a desert. Anything that once lived on or under the land disappears from the totally paved inner-city environment. However, cities are not just buildings and roadways. Most contain open space, parks, gardens, roadside tree plantings, and vacant lots. The natural environment is changed, but the transformed environment can provide a home for a great diversity of plants and animals. Exotic trees, shrubs, flowers, and grasses have been planted, along with a fair variety of native species. Native birds may benefit from urbanization. Studies in Berkeley showed that a greater variety and abundance of birds lived within the city than in the natural vegetation of the surrounding hills. Smaller mammals up to and including deer and coyotes may move into the open spaces of suburban areas. In time, some cities become urban woodlands, at the worst urban savannas, but in some areas, where tree canopies form a continuous cover, small urban forests.

Within the cities in the most densely populated sections, many aspects of the environment have recently improved. The cities of the nineteenth century were unsanitary places, often with unsafe water supplies, a lack of sanitary facilities, and an accumulation of garbage and refuse. Housing was commonly inadequate and unsafe. Diseases resulting from contamination of food or water were widespread. There was a fear of plague, which in fact did become endemic among wild rodent populations in some areas of the state, but has only rarely infected human beings. Malaria, encephalitis, and other mosquito-borne diseases were prevalent as a result of poor drainage. One of the arguments in favor of the introduction of eucalyptus trees from Australia, which were to transform the California landscape, was that they would help drain the marshes and swampy ground, and thus prevent malaria.

The first weak step taken by California to control pollution and improve the quality of water occurred in 1915, when a Bureau of Sanitary Engineering was established and all suppliers of domestic drinking water were required to obtain a permit from this bureau. Since no enforcement power was granted to the bureau, the requirement became meaningless. Very few communities assumed the task of treating and purifying waste water dumped into streams, bays, or the ocean. In the late 1920s and early 1930s, popular bathing beaches, such as the one at Santa Monica, were often lined with human feces. During the 1940s, with a greatly increased population, serious problems developed in several areas.

The Dickey Act of 1949 created nine regional water quality control boards which took on the responsibility of cleaning up the water supply. Sewage treatment plants have been constructed by most major communities and the dumping of raw sewage into water bodies has diminished. Yet the cost of constructing facilities which can discharge decontaminated water is enough to slow up progress. Even those which have been completed are subject to malfunction, such as resulted in 1979 when San Jose's treatment plant discharged sufficient quantities of raw sewage and chemical contaminants into San Francisco Bay to wipe out temporarily the normal aquatic life in the area affected. There are other ways to approach this problem—using less water, generating methane gas as an energy source, and producing useful fertilizer from human wastes—but these require separation of sewage components to eliminate toxic materials, decentralization of sewage facilities, and a reorganization of agricultural land-use practices. Under circumstances where taxpayers show increasing unwillingness to meet public costs, they may not be possible to achieve.

Before World War II, southern California was noted for its clear, dry air. Along with its unusually sunny weather, the favorable atmosphere led to the establishment of the moving-picture industry in Hollywood and in addition made the region a haven for people suffering from respiratory ailments. One of the world's most important astronomical observatories was constructed on Mount Wilson, overlooking Pasadena, and later the world's largest telescope was established at Palomar Mountain in San Diego County. In those days electric railway systems provided cheap, clean transportation for most of the region's citizens. But a nemesis had already arrived. The automobile industry joined with the petroleum industry to kill off the energy-efficient, nonpolluting electric railways and replace them with diesel-fueled buses. As Barry Commoner has pointed out:

> By 1949, General Motors had been involved in the replacement of more than 100 electric transit systems with GM buses in 45 cities including... Oakland... and Los Angeles. [In that same year] General Motors, Standard Oil of California and Firestone Tire Company, among others, were convicted in Chicago Federal Court of having criminally conspired to replace electric trolleys with gasoline or diesel-powered buses. General Motors was fined $5000, and its treasurer, who had participated in the dismantling of the $100 million Los Angeles trolley system, was fined $1.[1]

In the 1940s a new atmospheric phenomenon was described from Los Angeles, photochemical smog. The air had turned yellow and hazy and smelled bad. The smog was not much different from the old "killer fogs" that had plagued London for centuries. But where the London fog was filled with sulfur dioxide, resulting mainly from the widespread use of high-sulfur coal in space-heating and factories, the Los Angeles smog was derived mostly from the tail pipes of automobiles. It was a rich mixture: deadly carbon monoxide (47 percent of air pollution by weight), hydrocarbons in great variety, nitrogen oxides, which in turn join together to create ozone, and peroxyacyl nitrates (PANs). In the late 1940s Los Angeles responded to the threat by prohibiting backyard burning of vegetation and trash and by requiring factories to clean up the effluent which once poured out of smokestacks. The city required air-pollution control devices on automobiles, and the state passed laws to control automobile emissions. The standards have become increasingly strict, but the numbers of automobiles have grown to many million. In 1979 Los Angeles experienced its worst smog in several decades. The entire basin was covered with a dense brown haze, which spilled over mountain passes into the Mojave Desert. School children were kept indoors and not allowed to play. People were asked to stay home and try not to breathe too much. Smog is injurious to human and animal health. It also hurts plants. In the early 1970s a million ponderosa pine trees in the San Bernardino National Forest, eighty miles east of Los Angeles, had been damaged by smog. Crop losses in California from air pollution were reported in 1970 to have reached 25 million dollars. Many agricultural enterprises have been driven from the Los Angeles basin, not just by the spread of housing, but by smog. Meanwhile, the best possible smog-fighter, the old electric transit system, had been dismantled. The cost of replacing it would run into the billions of dollars. The Los Angeles people have shown a certain willingness to go down with their motor cars and freeways, fighting for the last drop of gasoline, and are reluctant to use public transportation. One cannot really blame them. The entire city has been built on the assumption that motor cars are forever. Without one a person can feel lost and helpless.

Smog is not just a southern California blight. Other cities around the world are in worse shape than Los Angeles, but smog is a serious menace to health nonetheless. If one flies over California during a period of temperature inversion, when air is trapped near the ground, the prevalence of smog over the Central Valley, the San Francisco Bay area, Sacramento, and other urban areas is painfully obvious.

The original Californians were faced with pollution problems resulting from human and animal manure. After European settlement, such deposits were mixed with a greater variety of pathogenic bacteria and viruses. With increasing sanitation, this kind of problem diminished, health was better, and life spans grew longer. Meanwhile, with the coming of mining and industry, new problems of pollution arrived. Wastes from mines, mills, and factories contained an increasing variety of toxic substances—heavy metals which accumulated in plant and animal tissues, sulfuric and other acids, toxic dyes and paint compounds, and such. After World War II new organic chemicals were added—polychlorinated biphenyls (PCBs) among them— which also had an ability to accumulate along ecological food chains and endanger animal life and human health. The automobile made its growing contribution, including dangerous amounts of lead. The first nuclear explosions that ended World War II were followed by a series of bomb tests in the atmosphere and underground. These brought new kinds of pollution from radioactive isotopes which emitted radiation harmful to living tissues. Arguments began then and continue to the present concerning the levels of radiation to be considered dangerous.

In an effort to harness nuclear power for useful purposes, California's first nuclear plant started operation in 1957 at Vallecitos in Alameda County, followed in 1963 by a Humboldt Bay nuclear power plant with a generative capacity of 70,000 kilowatts. During its first year of operation, it produced enough electricity to serve more than a hundred thousand homes. Almost no opposition was expressed to either plant since there was little public awareness of the problems of nuclear power plants—leaks of radioactivity to air or water, the peril of accidents, or the problems of storing dangerous wastes. The story was different, however, when the Pacific Gas and Electric Company decided to build its third plant, with a generative capacity of 325,000 kilowatts, on Bodega Head in Sonoma County. This area happened to be of great aesthetic, recreational, and scientific interest. It also was situated virtually on top of the San Andreas Fault. Since this fault line is not inconspicuous, one can only wonder in retrospect why PG&E chose this location. In the ensuing battle to prevent construction of the plant, the California public became aware of the hazards of nuclear plants, particularly in relation to earthquake faults. They also learned how to fight against them and win. PG&E announced in December 1964 that it had withdrawn from the struggle. Although two nuclear power plants, one at San Onofre and the other at Rancho Seco near Sacramento, were subsequently to come into operation, construction of a proposed plant at Sun Desert in the Mojave was prevented by state authorities, and there is serious doubt if the plant constructed at Diablo Canyon near San Luis Obispo will be allowed to operate. As of early 1980, California is not heavily committed to nuclear power.

The most serious poisoning of the California environment after World War II came from the agricultural sector of the economy. Farmers had always been plagued by insect pests, as well as by a variety of plant diseases, many of them rusts and smuts caused by fungi. Weeds of many kinds have been competitors with domestic plants since agriculture began. Synthetic organic pesticides, including the organochlorines such as DDT and organophosphates, of which parathion is a dangerous example, were brought on the market. Two potent new weed-killers—2,4-D and 2,4,5-T—also came on the market and were picked up for use on farms, rangelands, and forests. Initially these materials were but little-tested for their harmful effects upon organisms other than the designated "pests." Much of the early research in this direction was carried out by wildlife biologists who were concerned with the numbers of dead birds, fish, amphibians, and other animals found around the areas that had been sprayed with pesticides. The results of this research were brought to public attention in 1962 when Rachel Carson published her best-selling book, *Silent Spring.* Then began a long series of efforts by concerned people to force administrative agencies, legislatures, and courts to order the discontinuation of dangerous chemicals. DDT and some of its relatives were finally brought under control, but meanwhile new chemicals were being discovered and used faster than they could be tested for environmental effects. In 1976 between 252 and 290 million pounds of insecticides and herbicides were used in California to control weeds and insects.

DDT and its relatives have detrimental effects upon fish-eating or other carnivorous birds. The California brown pelican, a most conspicuous species along the California coast, went into a decline in the late 1960s. The one remaining breeding colony, on Anacapa Island off Oxnard, showed a decreasing production of young. Eggs that were laid were soft-shelled or lacked a shell altogether, and could not be hatched. Other sea-birds and marsh birds showed similar effects. A culprit was found in the form of the Montrose Chemical Company in southern California. It was engaged in DDT production and was allowing effluent from its factories, containing abundant quantities of DDT, to flow into coastal waters where it entered food chains and finally reached the brown pelicans. When this source was brought under control by action from the State Department of Fish and Game, pelicans began to recover, and in 1979 they managed to produce a record crop of young during a prolonged breeding season.

Elsewhere, the more pervasive use of DDT and its relatives affected the hawks and eagles. The bald eagle, golden eagle, peregrine falcon, and prairie falcon were among those harmed, with those feeding on fish or sea birds hit the hardest and joining the list of endangered species. The giant California condor, reduced to small numbers already, was found to be contaminated with pesticides. Still, it was not so much the decrease of wildlife, but the threat to human health that has brought action.

As the struggle to clean up pollutants in the environment continues, gains are made as the use of serious pollutants is reduced or eliminated. But each year thousands of different chemicals pour from the factories into the air, the soil, and the waters of California. What their ultimate effects will be no one really knows. The irony is that we cannot really wait to find out if they are truly dangerous since it could then be too late. It has been argued that the responsibility should be on the manufacturer to prove that they are not.

CHAPTER SEVEN

For Better or for Worse

N O PARTICULAR DATE in the history of California can one assign to mark the beginning of the environmental movement. A concern for the environment has always been here. Indians did not express a concern until they saw the damage that the white man could do, but then some of their spokesmen became eloquent. The Spanish colonists had their leaders who were concerned with the cutting of trees and the burning of the forests. Even the early settlers from the United States included those who were outspoken about the changes that seemed unfavorable to man and nature. But the majority of settlers were concerned with making a living rather than living with the land. They were more interested in acquiring riches than with enriching the earth that was supporting them.

As California moves into the 1980s, its people are perhaps better off than they deserve to be. Despite the war against nature that has raged for a century and a half, nature has held out, ready to come back wherever given half a chance to do so. On the most devastated lands, some weeds will grow, then a bird or two will move in, insects will colonize, and the process of regeneration and restoration will be under way. Even in the heart of gold rush country, the hydraulic "diggings" are being naturally restored. The forests have not come back, but they are the homes for stunted trees and cranberry bogs and the little fly-trapping sundews that could not have grown there in the days of the forests. The efforts of those who have sought to protect and conserve the wild California that they knew have brought success. They have fought a battle that is never won despite victories in the courts or legislature, for the opposition retreats but does not surrender and is always preparing a new assault. Half of the state has *not* been left wide open for exploitation, but is protected by some federal or state agency. On the other half a large percentage—and it would be interesting to discover how large—is in the hands of people who care for the land.

Many turning points have occurred in California history when one can say that the movement toward conservation, or environmental protection, gained impetus. The most recent came in the 1960s and had its roots in the spirit of rebellion that was sweeping the land. Many of those who fought against racism and marched for freedom in the South, or those who put their lives or future careers on the line to oppose the war in Vietnam, joined with others who saw as the principal issue the pollution and destruction of the American environment. The environmental movement gained a following and momentum that was not present before. Ecology became a catchword, and a sweeping change in public awareness took place. Many felt that concern for the environment came into being at that time, but its roots lay farther back in history.

Some of the changes in the protection of California's wildlife have already been discussed. The conservation movement by the 1930s had gained momentum; management and restoration by the 1950s were well under way. The tule elk, reduced to a small remnant herd, were restored to many parts of their original range. Moved from Kern County to the Owens Valley, they increased to levels where they did serious damage to ranches and farmlands. Hunting was instituted to keep numbers in check, but as a result of public pressure, this practice was halted and the elk were transplanted to areas they had once occupied—to Marin, Contra Costa, Santa Clara, and Merced counties. Meanwhile, the Roosevelt elk have increased to an estimated two thousand animals in the northwestern part of the state, and Rocky Mountain elk, not native to California, number nearly a thousand animals located in four separate areas. The pronghorn antelope has been brought back from its low point in the 1930s. In northeastern California, nearly five thousand animals now support a limited amount of hunting, and a small herd has been reestablished in Mono County. The bighorn sheep have also come back in some areas with numbers approaching five thousand.

Exotic species have been introduced into California, and some of these have been established for so long that many think of them as natives. The ring-necked pheasant from Asia is now the most conspicuous game bird in the Central Valley. The wild turkey from the eastern United States has been moved to California and has occupied the oak woodlands. The chukar partridge from India is a well-established resident in the sagebrush and desert areas. These species join a gallinaceous bird fauna still dominated by six native species of quail and grouse.

California's fish populations have changed from native to exotic as a result of the modifications of the state's water system from free-flowing streams to one dominated by reservoirs and irrigation channels. Of the 19 species considered to be game fish, and occupying warm waters, only one, the Sacramento perch, is native. All the others—bass, bluegills, sunfish, crappie, catfish, and bullheads—have been introduced in an effort to "improve" the fisheries. Species which fishermen do not prefer have also been brought into California and have done well— among them the carp, goldfish, and tench. Most of the sea-run fishes in California are native, but the striped bass and the shad are exotics which are now thoroughly at home in the state.

For the native species of fish, one cannot be as optimistic as for the native land animals. Artificial production from fish hatcheries helps to maintain moderate levels of salmon, sea-run trout, and fresh-water trout. Restoration of California's fisheries depends ultimately on changes in the management of the state's water resources and on greater attention to the protection of watersheds. There is still a long way to go before a reasonably high level of productivity will be achieved. In 1979 the Resources Agency of California launched a new program to restore natural spawning grounds. If successful, there should be great improvement in the waters still available to sea-run fish. The agency does not plan, however, to remove the dams.

The stewardship over California's fish and wildlife resources has rested officially with the state Department of Fish and

Game. The Fish and Game Commission determines policy for the department and establishes the regulations. However, considerable authority over endangered species, marine mammals, and offshore fisheries is now in federal hands as a result of various acts of Congress. The California legislature, from time to time, takes an active role in wildlife protection, overriding the commission to provide protection for mountain lions or to set conditions governing the hunting of deer. Traditionally, the public constituency for fish and wildlife has been the sportsmen and women of California, those who like to hunt or fish. For the most part, these people are a conservation-minded group who have been willing to restrict their own pursuit in order to enable wildlife populations to recover and become securely established. With the new environmental movement, however, has come a politically active constituency of people who do not like to hunt or fish, who may actively oppose sport hunting (although not usually sport fishing), and who want attention paid to the protection and restoration of "non-game" wildlife. Their ideas have caused a shift in the activities of the Department of Fish and Game and in the sources of funding. Although the main effort still goes toward protecting and restoring game species, a significant amount of resources is now directed toward endangered species of all kinds—reptiles, amphibians, song birds, wild plants—as well as the establishment of ecological reserves which can protect a spectrum of species. Funding no longer comes solely from the sale of hunting and fishing licenses, but from a variety of sources, including the general treasury. A new era of attention to the totality of wild nature, rather than just a few favored species, has started. One hopes it will not be short-lived.

It is not so easy to write about significant gains in the management of the state's grazing lands. The elimination of grazing from the national parks, and its control in the national forests, did much to restore the range in those areas. The large area of public domain that remained after these reserves were established had been overgrazed until 1946 when the federal Bureau of Land Management was established. This agency has begun to restore the ranges under its control, but the task has not been easy. On private lands the biggest factor leading to range restoration has been the increase in the prices paid for livestock and their products. Better prices have led to improved husbandry and management in many areas. But there is still a profit to be made in overgrazing and drought can wipe out the gains bought with years of conservative use on even the best-managed rangelands. The state Department of Conservation is concerned about overgrazing of rangelands and regards it as a major problem. In a detailed report it noted in 1979 that the

> central coastal rangelands have been shown by the California Department of Forestry to be one area of the State that is consistently subject to overgrazing. . . . Overgrazing of rangeland is creating accelerated water and wind erosion problems resulting in deteriorating range conditions [in the Sierra foothills]. . . . Studies have shown that range quality of the Mojave Desert is deteriorating under sheep grazing and offroad vehicle pressures. Grazing and trampling reduces plant cover and disrupts the soil surface, promoting wind erosion.[1]

There is still a long way to go to restore the conditions that could exist today. It is probably impossible to bring back the high productivity that existed in Indian times.

A new onslaught on the rangelands and on the dry and fragile ecosystems from sand dunes along the coast to high mountain meadows has developed since the 1960s with the growing popularity of off-road vehicles (ORVs), notably motorcycles and jeeps. In areas like the Mojave Desert that were once considered wild and remote, these vehicles have destroyed vegetation and animal life, caused severe wind erosion, and created channels to be turned by water erosion into gullies. In the south coastal mountains, heavy use by ORVs has eaten through soil into the underlying serpentine rock in some areas. Asbestos fibers released from this rock are carried by wind to make these areas dangerous to human beings because of the cancer-causing propensities of these fibers. Since ORV users are numerous, well organized, and politically influential, efforts of public agencies to control them have not been overly successful. But the scarcity and cost of gasoline may help officials do their duty as fewer people travel to the desert areas.

Undoubtedly a turning point for forest management came in the early part of the century when Gifford Pinchot and his colleagues helped Theodore Roosevelt establish the national forest system and convey to the public an idea of conservation. To followers of the Pinchot school of thinking, forests could be managed, and not just reserved, so that they yielded crops of timber, range forage, water, wildlife, and fish on a sustainable basis, taking advantage of the natural reproductive capacities of living organisms and enhancing the production and survival of young by management techniques. The idea that living resources could be used and still maintained was not new, but in its application to wild plants and animals it was a new approach. The idea of conservation as "wise use" became established in America. However, it encountered opposition from those who saw that a managed forest is different from a wild forest, that a primeval forest is too complex an entity to be easily restored when once disturbed. These critics were to follow a principle later stated by Aldo Leopold that the recreational value of wildlife (or a wild area) is inversely proportional to the management effort expended upon it.[2]

The national forests were to be managed not just on the principle of "sustained yield," but also on that of "multiple use." They were to serve all the people, producing the variety of resources of which they were capable. This policy suffered in time from the pressures and demands of the would-be forest users—those who wanted timber, range forage, water supply, or outdoor recreation. By 1979 a citizens' committee established by the Resources Agency of California reported that the Forest Service had gone too far and was in fact favoring timber production at the expense of other resources and values. In many national forests, stated the committee, the construction of dams and reservoirs had taken precedence over all other uses. Although those who manage the national forests, the public domain, and other multiple-use areas hark back to the dogmas of Gifford Pinchot and Theodore Roosevelt, it is doubtful if either of those men could have foreseen the massive onslaughts on the public lands made possible by the technological-industrial advances of the last three decades. The idea of multiple use and sustained yield of national forests, as originally put forward, was oriented more to the maintenance of healthy forest-based communities located in and near the national forests than to the enrichment of multinational corporations headquartered thousands of miles away. Roosevelt and Pinchot did not foresee the replacement of natural forests with high-yielding, single species stands of genetically selected stocks made possible by recent scientific and technological advances. Had they been able to do so, the arguments between Gifford Pinchot and John Muir might have been less rancorous.

On private timber lands, including most of the redwood and douglas-fir forests of the coast, the owners were not committed to either multiple use or sustained yield. Companies that wanted to stay in business over the long run were forced to encourage reforestation of logged-over lands in order to supply timber for the future. Companies which wanted a good public image or feared state or federal take-over of their lands made a point of encouraging recreational use of their property. They also pointed to public benefits in the form of wildlife and fisheries to be derived from their systems of management. However, when the chips were down, as they were in the 1960s and 1970s over the issue of creating a Redwood National Park, the timber companies demonstrated that they could be ruthless in their disregard for public interests and values. Logging was carried out deliberately in areas that the government hoped to purchase and where it would endanger redwood groves that were in public ownership.

In an effort to discourage destructive logging practices as well as to encourage citizens to protect forests and grow trees, the state legislature passed the Forest Taxation Reform Act of 1976. Essentially this law removed the tax incentive to cut trees by shifting the basis of taxation from an assessment of the value of standing timber to one based on yield. Taxes were only paid on the value of timber cut, not on trees left standing. The act further provided tax relief for private landowners who were not previously concerned with forestry. By creating "timberland preserve zones," landowners who were willing to commit their lands to the production of timber and who would agree to protect the growing stock would have their land tax bills reduced by the county tax assessors.

In 1979 the Resources Agency of California devoted much attention to tree production as one approach to solving the energy problems resulting from the decreasing quantity and high costs of petroleum. A Renewable Resources Investment Fund has been proposed to raise $35 to $45 million for reforestation, $170 to $250 million for wood/biomass energy development, and $6 to $7 million for urban forestry in order to bring tree production back within the city limits. At the same time, the federal government was asked to restore the 317,000 acres of California national forests that are badly in need of replanting and the much larger area that is poorly stocked with commercially useful tree species.[3] This indicates that there is a growing will to achieve balanced management of forest lands, and there is no reason to doubt that the 1980s will see marked improvements.

One of the landmark decisions of the 1960s was the passage of the federal Wilderness Act of 1964. It placed over nine million acres of National Forest Land in a Wilderness Preservation System and directed public land management agencies to review their holdings for further additions to this system. To 1979, an additional 6.1 million acres of National Forest land had been put in the Wilderness preserves. In 1972 the Forest Service completed its first roadless area review (RARE I) and then started on a second review (RARE II) which was completed in 1979. At that time twenty areas in California's national forests containing more than two million acres were included in the wilderness system, and two additional "primitive" areas were awaiting congressional action for inclusion. The Forest Service RARE II proposal suggested that an additional 750,000 acres be included, and that an additional large area be given further study. This proposal met with little approval from the public and private groups which favored more wilderness, and perhaps even less from the development-oriented people who wanted to build roads and use the resources of these wild areas. The state of California proposed that 1,450,000 acres be given immediate wilderness status. Conservation groups wanted still larger areas of wilderness to be proclaimed.

The wilderness controversy has once again focused attention on the policy of multiple use. Many foresters maintain that a wilderness designation removes the national forests from "multiple use," while others who favor wilderness emphasize the point that only destructive and damaging uses are prohibited, and wilderness areas still serve to produce water, watershed protection, wildlife, fish, recreation, and range forage. Although no decision can please everybody, it is apparent that areas reserved as wilderness are at least potentially available for other uses if circumstances change in the future. Those areas that are removed from wilderness status and opened for development cannot be recreated into wilderness—at least not the type of wilderness that is now in existence.

The future of California's wild lands in the 1980s and beyond continued to be affected by a decision of the 1870s which has had severe environmental consequences. This decision, the federal Mining Law of 1972, gives preference to mineral exploitation on public lands over any other uses and values. For hardrock minerals, miners or mining companies can stake claims on marketable ore bodies and receive free use of the land and resources in the claim area. By performing a hundred dollars worth of work per year, the claim can be maintained indefinitely. It is apparent that no plans for multiple use, sustained yield, wilderness or other combination of management and protection of the environment can hold up if any individual or corporation happens to discover marketable ores on the land. Revision of this archaic law has been resisted by mining interests which can exert considerable political pressure. Its revision, however, must be given priority for the 1980s since there is risk of losing much of what now appear to be environmental gains.

The problems relating to California's forests, rangelands, and wild species seem relatively easy to solve compared to the much more serious ones associated with water development, agriculture, and the urban-industrial-transportation complex.

Some of the issues associated with water development have been discussed in Chapter Five. Leaving aside the social inequities connected with the ownership of farm land and the public subsidy of water delivery for irrigation, there are other matters which are of concern for the environment. One is the massive energy subsidy required by commercial agribusiness. It is estimated that in this farming system it requires from seven to ten or more calories of energy (other than free sun energy) to produce and deliver one calorie of food to the table. Most of this comes from fossil fuels, petroleum primarily. Since other agricultural systems have a reverse ratio and can deliver ten to twenty or more food calories for each nonsolar calorie of energy input, it is apparent that a serious imbalance has developed. To this must be added the energy consumed by the water delivery systems under the Central Valley Project and the State Water

Project. Despite the generative capacities of the hydropower installations of the big dams, the water systems consume more energy than they produce. According to the *California Water Atlas:*

> Under ultimate project water deliveries, in fact, hydroelectric power plants on the State Water Project will generate only 40 percent of the estimated 12 billion kilowatt-hours per year the State Water Project will require by the year 2000; the rest will have to be obtained from other sources.[4]

Since the "other sources" have been fossil-fuel-fired, or to a minor extent, nuclear, power plants, they can be a serious cause of environmental disruption. Adverse environmental effects are associated with the mining of coal and oil shale, with the transportation of fuel, with power plant location, and the by-products of fuel combustion. Not the least of these is likely to be the growing level of carbon dioxide in the atmosphere resulting from fossil-fuel combustion. This has a high probability of bringing on adverse climatic change.

Agriculture in California has been water-wasteful, with nearly half of the state's total irrigated acreage now producing either crops with unusually high water needs, such as rice, or crops to be consumed by livestock. The practice of growing crops to feed domestic animals exaggerates the waste of energy in the agricultural system, since the subsidy of perhaps seven calories of fossil-fuel energy needed to produce each calorie of plant food must be multiplied five or ten times when these are fed to domestic animals to yield calories of meat, milk, or other animal products.

In addition to the waste of water and energy, the continuing input of agricultural chemicals leads to new problems. Those related to pesticides have been discussed, but the fertilizers themselves, nitrates and phosphates, not only are part of the energy subsidy, but also become pollutants of air and water. At the same time that factory-produced or -processed chemicals are being used wastefully on the farms, natural organic fertilizers are being treated as "wastes." Disposal of these organic materials from animal feed lots and city sewers has resulted in either serious water pollution, or in expensive treatment methods to prevent such pollution. Yet the same sewage could be a source of energy (methane gas) and of chemical nutrients for agricultural soils, thus reducing energy demands in both the urban and agricultural area.

It would appear that the greatest environmental challenge for the remainder of the twentieth century will involve, first, the development of a conservation-oriented agriculture which will be sparing in its use of water and imported energy, and will make maximum use of nutrients recycled from urban centers. With such development there would not only be less need for additional dams and aqueducts, but also a shift from an energy-consuming to an energy-producing use of water and agricultural land. Second, but associated with the agricultural transformation, is the need for restructuring urban-industrial systems. This has been, of course, a continuing process in California since the first Spanish pueblos took shape. Its new direction must be toward maximum use of nonpolluting, renewable energy sources, and toward recycling and reuse of all of those by-products of human activity which we now consider wastes.

For the long term human activities must be brought into better balance with environmental realities—they must become ecologically sustainable. California has little choice but to make the changes necessary to accomplish this. Without these changes the present systems of land and water use are likely to experience growing and more severe malfunctions with consequent adverse effects on human well-being. The move toward a conservation-oriented way of life need not bring hardship and can produce great rewards. California was one of the most favored lands on earth when it was first discovered. It can become that again.

NOTES

CHAPTER ONE

1. Phil C. Orr, "Radiocarbon Dates from Santa Rosa Island," *Santa Barbara Museum of Natural History Bulletin No. 2* (1956), 1–9.

2. William L. Kahrl, ed., *The California Water Atlas* (Sacramento: Governor's Office of Planning and Research, 1979), 17.

3. Paul S. Martin, "The Discovery of America," *Science* CLXXIX (1973), 969–974. For an opposite point of view, see M. A. Baumhoff and R. F. Heizer, "Post-Glacial Climate and Archaeology in the Desert West," in *The Quarternary of the United States* (Princeton, N.J.: Princeton University Press, 1965), 697–707.

CHAPTER TWO

1. Joseph Grinnell, Joseph Dixon, and Jean Linsdale, *The Fur-Bearing Mammals of California* (2 vols., Berkeley: University of California Press, 1937), I, 61.

2. *Ibid.*, 70–71.

3. *Ibid.*, 76.

4. Tracy I. Storer and Lloyd P. Tevis, *The California Grizzly* (Berkeley: University of California Press, 1955), 217:238.

5. Burton L. Gordon, *Monterey Bay Area: Natural History and Cultural Imprints* (2nd ed., Pacific Grove: Boxwood Press, 1977), 55.

6. *Ibid.*, 58.

7. Anita M. Daugherty, *Marine Mammals of California* (3rd rev., Sacramento: Calif. Dept. of Fish and Game, 1979), 10.

8. Quoted in W. H. Ellison, *The Life and Adventures of George Nidever* (Berkeley: University of California Press, 1937), 44.

9. Malcolm Margolin, *The Ohlone Way: Indian Life in the San Francisco–Monterey Bay Area* (Berkeley: Heyday Books, 1978), 9.

CHAPTER THREE

1. Edwin Bryant, *What I Saw in California* (1848; Santa Ana: Fine Arts Press, 1936), 284.

2. *Ibid.,* 288.

3. *Ibid.,* 294.

4. George Hendry, "The Adobe Brick as an Historical Source," *Agricultural History,* IV (1931), 110–127.

5. W. H. Ellison, *The Life and Adventures of George Nidever* (Berkeley: Univerity of California Press, 1937), 76.

6. F. A. Silcox, "The Western Range," 74th Congress, 2nd Session, *Sen. Doc. 199* (1936), 1–69.

CHAPTER FOUR

1. Elna Bakker, *An Island Called California* (Berkeley: University of California Press, 1971), 252.

2. Quoted in C. Raymond Clar, *California Government and Forestry* (Sacramento: Calif. Division of Forestry, 1959), 8.

3. Harold H. Biswell, "Fire Ecology in Ponderosa Pine-Grassland," Tall Timbers Fire Ecology Conference, *Proceedings, No. 12* (1972), 73–74.

4. Quoted in Clar, *California Government and Forestry,* 16.

5. *Ibid.,* 30.

6. *Ibid.,* 64.

7. Peter Behr *et al., Today, Tomorrow: Report of Citizen's Committee on U.S. Forest Service Management Practices in California* (Sacramento: Calif. Resources Agency, 1979), 48–49.

CHAPTER FIVE

1. W. I. Hutchinson, *Water for Millions* (San Francisco: U.S. Forest Service, 1956), 4.

2. Richard G. Lillard, *Eden in Jeopardy* (New York: Alfred Knopf, 1966), 56–58.

3. *Ibid.,* 149–155.

4. R. T. Silverman, *Economic Report of the Governor* (Sacramento: Calif. Dept. of Finance, 1979), A-38–39.

5. Calif. Department of Conservation, *California Soils: An Assessment* (Sacramento: Dept. of Conservation, in press).

CHAPTER SIX

1. Barry Commoner, *The Poverty of Power* (New York: Bantam Books, 1972), 198.

CHAPTER SEVEN

1. Calif. Dept. of Conservation, *California Soils: An Assessment* (Sacramento: Calif. Dept. of Conservation, in press).

2. Aldo Leopold, *A Sand County Almanac* (New York: Oxford University Press, 1949), 169.

3. Huey Johnson, *A Prospectus for the Future* (Sacramento: Calif. Resources Agency, 1979), 15.

4. William L. Kahrl, ed., *The California Water Atlas* (Sacramento: Governor's Office of Planning and Research, 1979), 78.

SUGGESTED READINGS

A DEFINITIVE environmental history of California will perhaps never be written if only because the term *environment* covers such a wide range of fields of expertise. To begin to understand the natural setting of California, Charles L. Camp's *Earth Song* (Berkeley: University of California Press, 1952) will provide an introduction to the geology and palaeontology, with Arthur D. Howard's *Geological History of Middle California* (Berkeley: University of California Press, 1979) providing more recent geological concepts. Elna Bakker's *An Island Called California* (Berkeley: University of California Press, 1971) is a beautifully written account of vegetation and land forms, and a good guide to the ecology and natural history of the state. Joel Hedgpeth's revision of Edward F. Ricketts and Jack Calvin, *Between Pacific Tides* (3rd ed., Stanford: Stanford University Press, 1952) provides detailed information on the partly submerged, marine margins of the state and the species that live there. For the larger animals there are many field guides and natural history accounts; however, the series published by the California Department of Fish and Game—of which Alan Craig et al., *Endangered Wildlife of California* (Sacramento: n.d.), and W. P. Dasmann, *Big Game of California* (Sacramento: 1962), are illustrative—provides both historical information and descriptive accounts.

For information on the California Indians, A. L. Kroeber's *Handbook of the Indians of California* (1925; New York: Dover Publications, 1976) is a classic. For the purposes of examining environmental relationships, Robert F. Heiser and Albert B. Elsasser, *The Natural World of the California Indians* (Berkeley: University of California Press, 1980), and Malcolm Margolin, *The Ohlone Way* (Berkeley: Heyday Books, 1978), are particularly relevant.

For detailed information on the Channel Islands, Ralph N. Philbrick, ed., *Proceedings of the Symposium on the Biology of the*

California Islands (Santa Barbara: Santa Barbara Botanic Garden, 1967), is a good starting point. An account of that area in Spanish times is provided in W. H. Ellison, *The Life and Adventures of George Nidever* (Berkeley: University of California Press, 1936). Further accounts of California during Spanish and Mexican occupancy and the early United States period are in Richard Henry Dana, *Two Years before the Mast* (1940; Los Angeles: Ward Ritchie Press, 1964); Edwin Bryant, *What I Saw in California* (Santa Ana: Fine Arts Press, 1936); and Francis P. Farquhar, ed., *Up and Down in California in 1860–1864: The Journal of William H. Brewer* (Berkeley: Univeristy of California Press, 1949).

The changes that took place in California's rangelands are best described by Lee T. Burcham, *California Range Land* (Sacramento: Calif. Division of Forestry, 1957). A history of forest use and forestry practice is provided by C. Raymond Clar, *California Government and Forestry* (Sacramento: Calif. Division of Forestry, 1959).

California's unusual history of water use and management is covered in Remi Nadeau, *The Water Seekers* (New York: Doubleday, 1950), and Richard G. Lillard, *Eden in Jeopardy* (New York: Alfred Knopf, 1966). For the most comprehensive coverage of the California water story, however, William L. Kahrl, ed., *The California Water Atlas* (Sacramento: Governor's Office of Planning and Research, 1979), is unsurpassed.

California agriculture is discussed in another volume of this Golden State Series, Lawrence J. Jelinek, *Harvest Empire: A History of California Agriculture* (San Francisco: Boyd & Fraser, 1979). To understand the complicated story of pesticides and their effects on land and life, Rachel Carson's *Silent Spring* (Boston: Houghton Mifflin, 1962), is the best starting point. Problems related to California's land ownership are discussed in Robert C. Fellmeth, *Politics of Land* (New York: Grossman, 1973).

INDEX